# It's Your Money, Honey

D1132646

# It's Your Money, Honey

*A Girl's Guide to Saving, Investing, and
Building Wealth at Every Age and Life Stage*

## by Laura J. McDonald and
## Susan L. Misner

John Wiley & Sons Canada, Ltd.

**Library and Archives Canada Cataloguing in Publication**

McDonald, Laura, 1978-

It's your money, honey : a girl's guide to saving, investing, and building wealth at every age and life stage / Laura McDonald, Susan Misner.

Includes index.

Issued also in electronic formats.

ISBN 978-1-181332-8-6

1. Women—Finance, Personal. 2. Finance, Personal. I. Misner, Susan, 1971- II. Title. III. Title: Girl's guide to saving, investing, and building wealth at every age and life stage.

HG179.M3247 2012          332.0240082          C2011-906195-3

978-1-118-15748-0 (ePub); 978-1-118-15747-3 (Mobi); 978-1-118-15749-7 (ePDF)

**Production Credits**
Cover design: Adrian So
Cover photo credit: Thinkstock/Hemera
Interior design: Thomson Digital
Typesetter: Thomson Digital
Printer: Webcom

**Editorial Credits**
Executive Editor: Karen Milner
Production Editor: Jeremy Hanson-Finger

John Wiley & Sons Canada, Ltd.
6045 Freemont Blvd.
Mississauga, Ontario
L5R 4J3

2 3 4 5 WEB 16 15 14 13 12

ENVIRONMENTAL BENEFITS STATEMENT

**John Wiley & Sons - Canada** saved the following resources by printing the pages of this book on chlorine free paper made with 100% post-consumer waste.

| TREES | WATER | ENERGY | SOLID WASTE | GREENHOUSE GASES |
|---|---|---|---|---|
| FULLY GROWN | GALLONS | MILLION BTUs | POUNDS | POUNDS |

To the little golden girls in our lives who inspire us to
think big, work hard, build, and prosper.

*Molly, Sadie, Annie, Anya, and Linnéa . . . we love you!*

# Contents

# Disclaimer

The material provided in this book is being provided for information purposes only. Nothing contained herein is intended to provide personalized financial, legal, or tax advice. Nothing should be construed as an offer to sell, or a solicitation of an offer to buy a security, a recommendation for any product or service by Golden Girl Finance, the authors or expert contributors herein, or any associated third party, or a suggestion regarding the purchase, holding, or sale of securities. Readers should not act on any information herein provided or implement any financial strategy without first obtaining professional advice from their financial, legal, and/or tax advisors who are fully aware of their individual circumstances and the rules that apply in the appropriate province and/or state.

# Preface
## Why We Wrote This Book

*Every Girl Needs a Financial Best Friend*

GoldenGirlFinance.ca launched in July 2010 because like many women (and men), we were bored with traditional personal-finance talk. At the end of a long, tiring day, would you rather read about Brangelina or bank rates, boozy escapades or bond yields? To borrow the words of a certain handsome pop star, we wanted to bring a little sexy back . . . to finance (yes, finance). Or let's be serious—introduce it for the first time.

We wanted to make finance fun, fresh, compelling, and engaging. And we wanted to have fun while doing it. Because while we may have expertise, we love a good laugh, a good read, and a compelling story. We tell it like it is—just like you. And you know what? That's sexy.

Ultimately, through our website, through our voice, and now through this book, we will help you learn to *strut*; to walk that walk that signals confidence—in yourself, in your career, and in knowing that you've got your financial you-know-what together.

We're here to talk about women supporting women to grow in their careers and to grow in financial dominance. (We always did want to rule the world.)

We ask just one thing of you: wake up. Yes, wake up, ladies! You're *worth* so much more than you know. Adopt this mantra and don't let anyone tell you otherwise.

It's time to get tough about our finances, to become aware, and to get engaged. The financial community, the world at large, and we ourselves need to recognize the power we hold in our manicured hands. Because make no mistake, ladies, recognizing your power is the sexiest thing of all.

So let's get started . . .

# Introduction
# Turning Smart Girls Golden

*Finance and Females*

## Let's Start at the Very Beginning

We met at a dance class. A Storybook Ballet class, to be precise, for our pre-school daughters. Climbing out of minivans, each of us gripped the hands of little girls in baby pink leotards and elasticized slippers while juggling cellphones, juice boxes, and zip-lock bags of Cheerios (spilling out onto the pavement, of course). Our eyes met across the crowded parking lot. There was a faint recognition, a long-ago memory of double dates, child-free nights, and carefree days. But we digress. Though we had been acquaintances a decade or so ago, we had not seen one another since. And those child-free nights were *long* gone.

Over the intervening years, each of us had gone on to build our careers, get married, and manage busy households. That day in the dance-studio parking lot, Susan was corralling her two little girls and Laura shepherded three. Five daughters under the age of four. (That's right, you don't want to end up next to our families on a plane.)

As we caught up over cold coffee in take-out cups and commiserated over sleepless nights and harried schedules, something clicked. We knew we were made to work together.

Susan had climbed the corporate ladder to become a top wealth-management advisor. Yet she was dismayed at seeing so many of her female friends—intelligent, educated, capable women—intimidated by investment advisors, unsure of their own finances and wary of economic explanations.

She instinctively knew that someone with a female perspective needed to reach out from the financial industry. A source that would understand women's lingo, would never undermine their opinions, and would assure them that all questions are valid and worthy of a legitimate response. The default voice of finance need not be male, she reasoned. And while the topics are often the same, why not change up the dialogue?

Enter Laura. A successful entrepreneur, writer, and communications consultant, she was financially clueless. Between juggling her job, her clients, and her three young children, Laura was quite content to leave the financial planning up to her husband. And yet, for an educated woman who was used to running her own business as well as a household, that didn't quite feel right.

Flashback a few years: Laura is nine months pregnant, taking the streetcar to the hospital while in labour with her first child while her husband made the long commute home. Okay, so she wasn't *entirely* sure this was the real deal; babies *do* take *way longer* to pop out than those silly movies would suggest; and she secretly *enjoyed* possessing this little secret amidst unsuspecting passengers. But still—labour and public transport generally don't mix.

The issue that dogged Laura, however, was not "what if my water breaks all over this stranger and his sci-fi novel?" The question was why on earth she did not just take a cab. In fact, the reason she took the streetcar was that at 27 years old, she was plain broke. Not even $20 to her name. How could she have let this happen? Here's how:

- She was in the non-lucrative business of trying to build a career as an actress.

- Hubby paid the rent and they never got a joint bank account.
- Hubby had taken away her only credit card following a series of minor shopping indiscretions to "teach her a lesson" about spending what she didn't have.

As a result, Laura found herself in their new city, where her husband had been transferred for work, with no family and few friends, and only a debit card . . . with a single-digit balance. No cash for a taxi, no credit card, and a baby kicking away feverishly at her stomach.

Sometime during that fateful streetcar ride, Laura realized that a man should never be a financial plan. No matter how confidently you act, how much knowledge and savvy you possess, regardless of how much respect you command among your colleagues and clients, you can still quite easily find yourself radically, financially, out of control.

And yet, life happens. Not too many years later, with two more babies under her belt, Laura still had not completely conquered the financial stuff (three kids in three years does that to a girl!), and continued to leave it up to her husband. She knew she should at least participate in the financial planning, but when you know so little, where do you begin? What questions do you ask? And above all else, who has the time?

## The Female Economy

Clearly, Laura was not alone in feeling like she needed to get a grip on her financial circumstances and start taking control of what she owned—now and in the future. You see, women worldwide are becoming wealthier and more independent. Between 1980 and 2008, the number of women in the global workforce doubled to 1.2 billion. As of 2009, women controlled 27 per cent, or about $20 trillion, of the world's wealth. Better still, this figure is expected to grow by 8 per cent each year until 2014.[1] (High five, ladies!)

Just to put that in perspective, the "female economy" represents more than $5 trillion of incremental spending by women over the next several years.[2] This is larger than the growth potential for India's and China's consumer economies.

The consensus? We have so much power! You'd think that financial advisors and consumer-marketing groups would be eating these statistics up like candy and dying to get their money-hungry fingers on us gals and our growing bank accounts. Yet companies often miss the mark, thinking if they brand their products pink—*bam*—they've cornered the women's market.

Wake up, world! Not only do we think and react a lot differently than men (and not just in shades of pink), our lives follow much different paths than those of our brothers. Think about it:

- We earn less. Currently, a woman earns just 83 cents (some studies suggest even less) for every dollar earned by a man.[3] **Takeaway: Our dollars have to stretch further to achieve the same lifestyle.**

- We are in the workforce for a shorter period of time. Between maternity leave, part-time work, and caring for kids, parents (and, yes, husbands), we generally end up dipping in and out of the workforce throughout our careers. **Takeaway: We have smaller retirement savings and fewer earning years.**

[1] Peter Damisch, Monish Kumar, Anna Zakrezewki, et al. *Leveling the Playing Field: Upgrading the Wealth Management Experience for Women* (Boston: Boston Consulting Group, 2010), 1, http://www.bcg.com/documents/file56704.pdf

[2] Michael J. Silverstein and Kate Sayre. *Women Want More: How to Capture Your Share of the World's Largest, Fastest-Growing Market* (Boston: Boston Consulting Group, 2008), 1, http://www.womenwantmorethebook.com/documents/file21481.pdf

[3] Statistics Canada, "Why Has the Gender Wage Gap Narrowed?," 20 December 2010, http://www.statcan.gc.ca/daily-quotidien/101220/dq101220b-eng.htm

- Once we hit 65, a woman can expect to live until she is 86 (on average), about three years longer than a man.[4] **Takeaway: Our Botox funds (oops!), we mean retirement savings, need to last longer.**
- Many women spend more of their lives alone—either by marrying later in life, getting divorced, being widowed, or choosing to remain single. **Takeaway: We must be prepared to live self-sufficiently for a good chunk of our adult lives.**

But here's the silver lining. Women's rising influence in the economy is starting to shake things up. After decades (or even centuries) of mothers nagging daughters about getting married, finally, *finally*, in 2008, money replaced marriage as the number one topic of discussion between mothers and daughters. Thankfully today, 91 per cent of women surveyed said they are talking to family members about money.[5] Investing, saving, spending, and anxieties and concern over money are the top financial topics being discussed.

We'll raise a glass of Pinot after a long hard day to that.

## A Golden Idea

An idea began to emerge.

Clearly, we saw the need for a non-biased forum where women could talk to other women about finance, investing, and the market: finance for women by women. An approachable source that would appreciate women's unique challenges and address the life stages that women go through. Most critically, we saw the need to communicate to women in a manner that interests and engages them (and us)

---

[4] Statistics Canada, "Deaths," 23 February 2010, http://www.statcan.gc.ca/daily-quotidien/100223/dq100223a-eng.htm

[5] Women & Co and Citibank, "A Glimpse Into The SHE-conomy—Key Findings from Women and Affluence 2010: The Era of Financial Responsibility," https://www1.citibank.com/womenandco/docs/pdf/studies/survey2010.pdf

more profoundly than traditional financial media has done. After all, much of the discussion applies to both sexes, but the voice certainly need not.

And thus Golden Girl Finance was born, recognizing that too many smart women let their financial situations be ignored, swept under the rug, or dictated by others. And we're talking about capable women . . . who have master's degrees, manage a household of kids, run their own businesses, volunteer for the PTA, shovel the driveway, pump their own gas, and all in all, are your regular supergirls/supermoms/superwives/superwomen.

Through our website, newsletters, articles, events, and now this book, Golden Girl Finance strives to engage women to take a greater interest—and play a greater role—in those financial issues that affect their everyday lives and financial futures, and to rebrand finance with a decidedly feminine spin.

And, yes, we know you're not looking for a textbook on economics. Who has the time? We don't, and we're betting you don't either. (Let's be honest, if you have any downtime, you would probably rather read a fashion magazine, a cookbook, or the latest vampire fiction. We totally agree.)

You need accessible, compelling, relevant, and valuable financial and career information . . . that is actually entertaining to read.

Mission accomplished.

## So Here's How It Works

When you need that hit of financial savvy, we're here for you. You will find the content in this book organized according to life stages. After all, love it or hate it, your finances will affect or be affected by your relationships, your jobs, your dreams of success, your desire to start a family, and the lifestyle that you ultimately want to live. It all depends on your money and how you manage it.

We hope you will dip into this book time and time again, as a sort of financial survival guide. We will cover many stages of life—not all of which will apply to you—but which you might find useful when your daughter or niece comes to you for advice; or when your best friend confides that she is struggling with a financial decision (or a divorce). Because here's the thing . . . every girl needs a financial best friend. Be that friend!

Indeed, on the subway or in a waiting room, whenever you have a few minutes to learn something new, brush up for an upcoming life event, or react with confidence to another curveball unexpectedly thrown your way, we're here for you—just like you are for your friends. We hope this book will be a point of reference as you move forward with your life, your career, and your relationships; pages you can turn to (and return to) no matter where life leads you—through turmoil and triumph.

Above all, while this book will provide valuable information for the big moments in life, it also includes steps to easily integrate finance into your everyday life in a fun and engaging way—*and* how to make it social with a Golden Girl Finance Club of your very own (see the Discussion Guide at the end of this book). Because getting women *talking* about their finances is what we are all about.

## Your Entourage

To get you started, we've assembled a powerhouse group of experts to offer insight throughout this book, covering everything from business to law, financial planning to debt reduction, marriage to divorce. We've got you covered, babe.

Think of us like your personal board of directors. Why? Well, if we were at one of our events right now, we'd show you a photo of a woman getting a manicure. (Because that has *so* much to do with finance, right? Um, no.) The reason is because, like many of us, you probably saw your manicurist in the last month. (Don't hide those gel nails behind your back!)

Now, we're not going to argue the benefits versus costs of glamming up your digits (and feel free to replace manicure with the indulgent outsourcing of your choice), but we do want to throw this back at you: When did you last speak to your financial advisor? Or your lawyer? Or your accountant? (Do you even have one of each of these? And if so, do you personally and regularly correspond?)

We thought not.

Think about it this way: you have your hairstylist, your manicurist, your bikini waxer. Oh, and your masseuse, your naturopath, and that barista who makes your no-foam soy latte just the way you like it. The list goes on. While you may not have a personal assistant per se, we all have a team of excellent individuals who attend to our everyday needs, from the more important (your doctor) to the more mundane (those gel nails).

So why, ladies, don't you have a lawyer on that list? Or a smart accountant who knows the ins and outs of taxable income? Or a financial planner or wealth-management advisor who *you* vetted and trust?

Most of us are more than happy to have our more superficial needs covered, but we don't arm ourselves with powerful allies who can help us navigate life's uncertainties and challenges with confidence, knowledge, and from a position of strength. At Golden Girl Finance, we call it surrounding yourself with your *own* circle of financially savvy friends, and we suggest you do it before a life-altering event. This way, you'll be in a much better position to act quickly and with confidence, armed with guidance from individuals you already know and trust.

That said, until you assemble your real-life professional posse, we are ready, willing, and eager to help you. This book will get you armed and engaged. And above all else, inspire great things for your financial future.

## Fearless Legacies

And on that note, it really is about the future. Women, in particular, have strong legacy needs, whether they just graduated or just attended their granddaughter's graduation. They feel a continual push to build great families, careers, and communities; to be influencers in this world; and to leave a lasting legacy.

For us personally, our five little powerhouse daughters, now aged six and under, are our primary motivators. (Also our primary heartaches, primary pains in the neck, and primary objects of our undying adoration.)

We want our girls to grow up learning about financial matters with the same nonchalance and fearlessness with which they approach French, geography, and, currently, the monkey bars. We want them to enter adulthood confident about their ability to independently control their finances and make decisions based on their dreams, rather than their fears. And we want that same financial confidence, security, and stability for your daughters, nieces, and loved ones of all ages.

## It All Comes Back to the Name

We're about turning smart girls golden. *Golden Girl Finance.* Hmmm . . .

Of course we'd heard of the iconic 1980s television show, *The Golden Girls*, when we coined the name. And no, we are not trying to evoke the images of Bea Arthur and Betty White. (Though what's not to love about those brazen, ballsy, and independent babes? We dare you to suggest that Dorothy couldn't take any man down.) Nor were we trying to channel the two butt-kicking superheroines of the same name from the 1940s Marvel Comics universe. (Again, not that we mind the comparison. It's pretty cool.)

The truth is, there is something magical and inspirational about the term *golden girl*. A woman who turns everything she touches into success. A goddess with untold wealth, wisdom, allure, ambition, and power.

Most importantly, gold in the financial world is considered to be a "store of value," providing safety, security, and stability in tumultuous times.

Yup, young or old, a golden girl is holding her own, honey.

Just like us. Just like you. So let's do it, shall we?

Laura J. McDonald

Susan L. Misner

# 1

## The First Taste of Freedom

*Finance and Starting Out*

### If the World Is My Oyster, Where Is the Pearl?

Oh, hello, adulthood! Is it every bit as glorious and sophisticated as you dreamed it would be when you were 13?

Let's take stock. You can wear high heels every day *and* eat chocolate cake for breakfast (combine the two and you're on to something). You can leave the dishes in the sink, heap your bedding on the floor, and sip cocktails from fancy glasses (dirty ones, but nonetheless). You can play your music as loud as you wish. You can call a taxi, go to the airport, and fly to Paris. Well, theoretically anyway.

The reality is, you're probably wearing out your flip-flops, eating cereal for dinner out of a coffee mug, struggling to pay rent, and bemoaning the cost of luxuries, such as lattes, nightclub cover charges, and mobile-phone plans (what an expensive lifeline!).

Yes, the first harsh lesson of adulthood is that nothing is quite as sexy as it once seemed. Perhaps you find yourself longing for the days when all your income was *disposable*. (There's a reason you had the designer yoga pants while your mom walked around in the grocery-store knockoffs.) Living at home came with generous perks: a refrigerator full of groceries; unlimited Internet, cable, and phone service; possibly an allowance; and free rein to spend any (and all!) part-time job earnings on clothes, music, movies, and unlimited overpriced coffee treats. You may now start to realize that life under the tyranny of your parents definitely had its benefits.

Don't fret, sugar. Glory days will come again. You are at a fabulous stage of your life *right now*, positioning yourself for your place in the world. This is the time to try new things, test out your interests, and gain confidence in your abilities. The question is no longer, "What do I want to be when I grow up?" Rather, the question for you to consider is, "What would I like to try first?"

Gone are the days when a person studied for one trade or career and maintained that occupation for the rest of her life. Nowadays, an educated individual with creativity, resilience, and flexibility can look forward to an evolutionary career, where job opportunities and experience can lead you down exciting (and sometimes meandering) paths to a future you likely never even considered or, dare we say, dreamed possible. (In future years, when you are asked how you knew that meandering path would lead you to prosperity, you can just smile and say that you were being "strategic.")

And yet, you may actually be so overwhelmed by this multitude of choice that you're unable to take even one tiny step forward. How to choose a field of study? University or technical college? How do you balance school with real-life work experience? What about taking a gap year? Should you live with a roommate or stay at home a little longer?

The beauty of your life at this stage is that you really can't make a mistake. The goal now is to learn more about yourself and your values: what you can and cannot tolerate, what you excel at doing, and what you would definitely not enjoy doing over the long term.

Life is young, so enjoy it! But at the risk of sounding like old hags trying to rain on your parade, take it from us: the days may pass slowly, but the years move quickly. Planning for the future—and a financially sound one—is a great thing. Consider yourself lucky: you are in the optimal time of your life to start having a *massive* impact on your future wealth. Forget waiting for Prince Charming. The fairytale is *yours* . . . if you start now. So let's look at some of the choices and implications of these glory years together, shall we?

---

 **LIFE LESSON: KEEP THE DOORS OPEN**

Now is the time to open doors, not close them. When faced with a major decision, consider whether the opportunity will advance you toward more options or limit your future choices. Let a decision come to a definitive yes-or-no point before making your choice. Use your time to do research and get advice from people you trust. Remember that circumstances can change quickly during this stage of your life, so you might feel differently in a week, a month, or even a year.

---

## Your Own Roof, Your Own Rules

Finally, the days of "as long as you're living under my roof" are over and you can kick back and enjoy the sweet taste of freedom! Right? Well, almost. Freedom, of course, comes with responsibilities, not the least of which are rent and roomies. Consider the following tips.

## Renting Your First Place

- **Read your lease *thoroughly* before you sign it.** Know what costs you are responsible for covering, when your rent can be changed, how it must be collected, and what happens if payments are late.

- **Landlords can inquire about your credit rating,** so being responsible with your credit can make the difference between scoring a place you love, settling for something less, or finding yourself staying with Mom and Dad longer than you, ahem, hoped.

- **When renting on campus, many landlords will ask a student's family to guarantee their debt obligation.** This could make it difficult to rent decent accommodations if you can't provide such a guarantee.

- **Protect your security deposit.** Walk around your rental space before you sign the lease and make sure both you and your landlord record any existing defects before you sign off. You should both initial this list and attach it to each copy of the lease agreement.

- **Landlords really do check references.** By taking good care of a landlord's property, you can develop a reputation for yourself as a desirable tenant, with the good references to prove it.

- **Make sure you can afford to pay the rent for your place on campus even if you go back home over the summer.** Most landlords will insist on a full-year lease and it can be difficult to sublet when student housing floods the market during school break periods.

- **Budget for apartment contents insurance, a must for protecting your possessions.** Local police departments can vouch that when classes are over, student neighbourhoods are an easy target.

Many apartments are empty over the holidays, leaving televisions, gaming equipment, and computers as tempting targets for thieves.

## Living with Roommates

Roomies are a whole other concern. On the one hand, they could become your lifelong pals, inspiring annual reunions to reminisce, drink blue martinis, and tell inside jokes for the rest of your lives. On the other hand, they could steal your food, "borrow" your wine, and give their obnoxious boyfriend the spare key. Here are a few tips to keeping peace and financial order with a house-full of roomies:

- **Not all rooms in an apartment are created equal.** Some are larger, sunnier, have better closet space, or an ensuite bathroom. Have a conversation with your potential roommates about this to determine what the priority is for each of you *before* you set out looking. You can gain flexibility by having a diverse group of roommates—some who can pay more and others who are happier paying less in exchange for smaller digs.

- **Account for the regular monthly payments together.** Think rent, electricity, phone, cable, and Internet, to name a few. For costs that fluctuate, ensure each of you budgets for a monthly average so you don't find yourself with a shockingly high heating bill in the winter.

- **Grocery costs have been known to require United Nations intervention among roommates.** With a small group of roomies, you may choose to share staples (such as flour, sugar, coffee, tea, rice, pasta, dairy, ketchup, milk, and paper products), allowing each person to select more specific or "splurge" purchases for her own use. In larger groups, many opt for the "every woman for herself" policy, whereby everyone has their own dedicated shelf in the cupboard and refrigerator space.

- Read *Getting to Yes,* by Roger Fisher and William L. Ury, and learn the art of negotiation to keep the peace! This will come in handy when the last drop of communal milk is gone and you haven't even had your morning coffee yet.

- Make the most of parental visits. A trip to the grocery or bulk-food store with Mom or Dad can keep you in peanut butter and drink crystals for months.

---

 **HINDSIGHT**

*A note of caution: make sure that whatever your parents buy you— think the non-consumable stuff like kitchen utensils, Ikea couch, DVD player—is marked as yours in the end, even though all may be sharing in the enjoyment now. One former roomie assumed the furniture (paid for by my parents) in our shared apartment was to be split when we parted ways after graduating. Who knew I needed a pre-nup for college cohabitation?*

---

## The Value of an Education

Strolling across a sun-dappled lawn, a handsome guy offers to help you with your backpack. As you walk toward the library together, he casually asks whether you take a scientific or a Romantic view of the most recent environmental catastrophe. You recite a line from Poe and catch his admiring gaze . . .

Sounds idyllic, right? Even if your university experience runs more to calculus labs and beer gardens, college offers a rare opportunity to dedicate yourself to the world of ideas and the passion of learning. Post-secondary education gives you a chance to "learn how to learn," to be exposed to generations of critical thought, to advance your cognitive skills, and to formulate your own opinions in the face of traditional rhetoric.

Once you enter the workforce, you may never have this luxury again. But is it a luxury? Or is it a sensible investment to help you gain higher earning power in the future?

The return on the investment in securing a university degree is hotly debated, and as you can imagine, tough to quantify. A British study declared that a university degree adds, on average, £2,500 ($4,000) per year, or £100,000 ($160,000) over a 40-year career, compared to having no degree.[1]

Meanwhile, a U.S. Census Bureau study concluded that people with a bachelor's degree could expect to earn an average of $2.1 million throughout a 40-year working life, compared to $1.2 million for high-school graduates, amounting to an estimated premium of $22,500 per year. Those with doctoral and professional degrees fare even better, according to the study, earning an average of $3.4 million and $4.4 million respectively.[2]

Others, such as American political scientist and author Charles Murray, have argued that an undergraduate degree merely lets an employer know that you have perseverance and a certain level of intellectual prowess. (Which is not for nothing, as far as we're concerned.)

---

[1] Graeme Paton, "A University Degree 'is worth £2,500 a year'," *The Telegraph*, 7 December 2009, http://www.telegraph.co.uk/education/6754287/A-university-degree-is-worth-2500-a-year.html

[2] Jennifer Cheesman Day and Eric C. Newburger, *The Big Payoff: Educational Attainment and Synthetic Estimates of Work-Life Earnings*, U.S. Census Bureau, July 2002, http://www.census.gov/prod/2002pubs/p23-210.pdf

GOOD NEWS FOR GRADS

"The demand for university graduates in the last 20 years has been high: of the 1.5 million new professional and management positions created, 1.3 million were filled by university graduates. The increased demand is a direct response to the shift in Canada's labour market from a resource-based economy to a knowledge-based economy. However, the economy is in for a dramatic demographic shift over the next two decades. By 2030, the number of people over the age of 65 will double, while the 25–64-year-old population will grow by a mere 8 per cent. There will be a huge demand for professionals such as doctors, lawyers, accountants, and entrepreneurs."—From the Association of Universities and Colleges of Canada.[3]

## How on Earth Do I Pay for University?

There is no way around it—higher learning is expensive. Tuition and books alone will set you back thousands of dollars, at a time in your life when you're likely used to earning minimum wage. And the price is rising. By the year 2027, the cost (including living expenses) is estimated to reach more than $110,000 for an average four-year bachelor's degree.[4] Yikes! Here are some ways to finance your university years.

### The Bank of Parents

If you have parents or grandparents willing to bankroll your studies, consider yourself very fortunate. Send these kind benefactors regular

---

[3]The Association of Universities and Colleges of Canada, "University enrolment continues to climb," 28 October 2010, http://www.aucc.ca/media-room/news-and-commentary/university-enrolment-continues-to-climb
[4]CanLearn, Canadian Student Loans Program Directorate, Human Resources and Skills Development, http://www.canlearn.ca

reports from school. Call them, often. Invite them to your graduation ceremonies to share in your accomplishment. And even though you might have some grumpy moments in keeping up with their e-mails and phone calls, remember that they care about you enough to invest in your future.

As comedian Amy Poehler said in her commencement address to Harvard graduates in the spring of 2011, "[Your parents] have sacrificed so much for you and all they want you to do is smile and take a picture with your weird cousins. Do that for them. And with less eye-rolling, please."[5]

## Free Money

Whether you have help to pay for school or you are on your own, the best way to reduce the costs is by accessing free money. Yes, that's right—we're talking about scholarships, grants, and bursaries. All across your country or region, there are millions and millions (and did we mention, millions?) of dollars just waiting to find clever students like you. Here's what you need to consider:

A **scholarship** is an award recognizing academic excellence or other special achievement. In some cases, financial need may also be taken into account. Scholarship funds may cover the cost of tuition, books, as well as living expenses, or they may be a lump-sum payment.

A **bursary** is an award based on financial need. When applying for a bursary, you typically are required to supply a financial statement indicating your assets and expenses. Usually paid as a lump

---

[5] Amy Poehler, "2011 Harvard University Class Day Speech," *Harvard Gazette*, 24 June 2011, http://news.harvard.edu/gazette/story/2011/06/2011-harvard-university-class-day-speech-by-amy-poehler/

sum for a defined amount, bursaries often request that applicants meet certain geographic or demographic requirements.

A **grant** is any kind of financial award beyond scholarships and bursaries and does not require repayment. It may or may not require proof of financial need and may be any kind of cash prize or payment to cover costs.

Elite, high-profile government scholarships tend to be awarded on scholastic merit, athletic ability, or community involvement. There are also thousands, if not millions, of more obscure scholarships, bursaries, and grants offered by associations all over the world that often go unawarded due to a lack of applicants.

Can you call ducks? The Chick and Sophie Major Memorial Duck Calling Contest might have $2,000 for you. Are you over 178 centimetres (5 feet 10 inches)? The Tall Clubs International Student Scholarship could give you $1,000. Are you of Italian descent and living in Quebec? The Canadian-Italian Business and Professional Association of Montreal could have a bursary of more than $3,000 waiting for you!

Of course, you've got to play to win. Accessing all this free money requires some patience and diligence in filling out applications and often writing essays about yourself and how you will make the organization proud (you are so worthy!). So, buckle down and start writing.

Once you've got one essay down, you can certainly multi-purpose it for other applications. If it takes you 10 hours to write a fantastic essay for use with five applications, even if you only end up scoring one $1,000 award, that would still net you $100 an hour for your efforts. (Hey, no matter what you plan to study at school, it's going to be a while before you earn that kind of dough just for 60 minutes of your time.) So get busy, honey. Surely there is some free money out there with your name on it!

---

**WHEN CONTROL ISN'T COOL: PAVE AND PAY YOUR OWN WAY**

Although it might seem like a relief if Mom and Dad offer to foot the bill for your living expenses (rent, vehicle, credit cards, and so on), the reality of the matter is that all young adults need to learn how to stand on their own two feet. And the sooner, the better.

Not only can a lifestyle that is bought and paid for by someone else impact the ability for you to gain self-esteem, confidence, and competence from providing for your own needs, it can also, in some instances, lead to unhealthy control by others over your lifestyle and choices.

Remember this saying: "She who has the gold makes the rules." This needs to be *you*!

---

## Borrowed Money

If you can't get free money, borrowed money is the next best thing. Unfortunately, student or not, a loan is a loan and needs to be repaid at some point. There are two main types of student loans and it is important to know the difference before you sign on the dotted line:

### 1. Government Loans

These loans usually require that parents either sign off that they *won't* help you with your education costs or supply financial statements to demonstrate that they *can't* help you. The interest rate is often fairly reasonable and interest typically does not accrue until after you graduate if you're a full-time student. Depending on your circumstances, you can sometimes qualify for temporary interest relief, but this should be considered only as a last resort. If you can afford a new pair of shoes that you don't absolutely need, you should not apply for interest relief. That loan balance isn't going anywhere, so putting off paying it down is only going to make it costlier in the long run.

### 2. Bank Student Loans and Lines of Credit

Your parents may be required to co-sign with you in order to qualify for this type of financial assistance, and this is no small undertaking. Letting someone co-sign a loan for you is always a big deal and you should offer to sign a private agreement about what would happen if you should ever have trouble making payments. If you are late on a payment or in default, this can seriously damage your parents' credit rating.

Bank loans are typically stricter than those provided from the government. Often, interest accrues while you are still in school. With student lines of credit, the limit is typically decreased to meet the outstanding balance once you are out of school, so technically it's no longer a line of credit. This means that if you make a payment of $10,000, both the credit limit and the balance fall by $10,000. But what you really need to watch is the interest rate: if it is a variable rate, it will increase (or decrease) when the prime lending rate moves. Be sure to find out how high the rate is above the prime rate when you sign up and understand how much higher it could go. This is critical for understanding how your payments and loan balance could be affected in the future.

 **LIFE LESSON: STUDENT LOANS ARE SACRED**

Never, ever put the proceeds of a student loan into your bank account. Never park that money where your debit card can access it. A separate high-interest savings account (one where you need 24-hours' notice to make a withdrawal) works best. If you are going to take living expenses from the loan proceeds, pay yourself every two weeks, just like a paycheque, by setting up an automatic transfer from your high-interest savings account to your regular spending or chequing account. *No* exceptions, *no* advances (you will thank us later).

## The University of Life

If the thought of staying put in the same small college town day in and day out for the next four years is more than you can handle, consider these options to keep you focused on your studies while adding some adventure, excitement, and real-life experience.

- **Exchange programs**

  Most universities have programs that allow you to study at a university abroad for a semester. This is especially appealing to those who have chosen to save expenses by living at home. You get to expand your horizons without taking time off school or incurring the costs of full-time university abroad (not to mention the potential to learn a new language, experience a new culture, and see sights that you might otherwise not be able to experience).

- **Co-op work programs**

  It might take you a little longer to graduate, but co-ops are a great way to accumulate work experience and make contacts in your industry. This can be an extraordinary advantage, in terms of helping you to pay for your education as you go, having practical work experience that other students may lack, and scoring a job when you graduate.

## The Big-Name School—Is It Worth It?

If you have the means and the merit (top scores, clever girl!), you might wonder whether it's worth it to choose an Ivy League school or other prestigious university at home or abroad.

There is no question that a big name will look great on your resumé. A powerhouse school can give you access to resources and academia you might not otherwise find, as well as connect you with future movers, shakers, and leaders (just like yourself, of course).

However, these universities come at a steep price, not only for tuition, but also for accommodations and the stress of highly competitive admissions processes.

Think of it like buying a dress. Do you choose an haute-couture piece that will no doubt impress the fashion elites (while completely sabotaging your savings)? Or do you buy a less expensive, knock-off version in order to get the job done and stay on budget (just pair it with a statement necklace and no one will know the diff, right)? Alternatively, you may choose something in between. After all, if it's a dress for an important occasion, you will probably shop around to find a brand or boutique whose styles flatter your figure and suit your personality, even if that means choosing a relatively unknown local—and more reasonably priced—designer.

Along the same lines, smart girls *comparison shop* to see which school can deliver the best quality program for the course of study in which they are interested. Despite their reputations, top-name universities are not always ideal for all disciplines. Every school has its departmental strengths and weaknesses. Check the reputations of the professors in the department of your major or the quality of research being published. If you plan to study law or business, check with the firms you hope to be hired by, to see where their partners went to school.

Often the quality of instruction for an undergraduate degree is fairly comparable across the board. If you choose to do a master's or post-graduate program, a name university might become more important to you then.

Finally, don't forget the intangibles that can really define your university experience. Low student-to-faculty ratios, close-knit communities, strong extracurricular programs, proximity to home, work-study programs, and the general feel of the campus environment are all worth considering when determining the value of a school.

**GOLDEN RULE: SPLURGE VERSUS SAVE EDUCATION**

There are times when you can go generic and get exactly what you need for a lower price. And then, there are times to splurge a little on things that will make a difference in your life.

Use this approach to develop your education plan: go generic (or close to home) for your undergraduate degree and splurge on the best school you can once you've narrowed the focus of your studies and have a clear idea of the career direction you want to take. At this point, a school that specializes in your chosen discipline will give you access to the academics that will boost your opportunity to learn, as well as the career-advancing chance to network with fellow grad students. This mix of high-low spending should give you an ideal fit for your educational dollar.

## Take Advantage of the Little Windfalls

Living at home can make a huge difference to the cost of your education. The costs of university or college residence and meal plans can run more than $10,000 per year, and no, that's *not* including tuition. You may end up waiting years longer to purchase your first home—simply by choosing to live on campus rather than stay with your folks a bit longer. Choose wisely! When all of your friends are buying their starter homes, you could be staring at a student-loan balance that will force you to continue to pay someone else's mortgage in the form of rent—for a lot longer than you imagined. Continuing to live at home *just a little bit longer* while you go to school means that the money you save can be the down payment on *your* first home.

It all comes down to making good use of the little windfalls in life . . . and staying at home, while saving your cash, is a great example. Saving $15,000 to put toward your first home at age 25 could snowball into a home that you sell for a $50,000 profit five years later. By age 30, these earnings combined with your enhanced income could net you a new home that may be even bigger than the one you grew up in. And the snowball continues. It's a pretty cool thing (and way better than a lazy roommate, pint-sized dorm room, or a closet full of bar-star clothes and strappy bejewelled sandals that you'd no longer be caught dead wearing).

## To Work or Not to Work, That Is the Question

When your school calendar is packed with homework and assignments, it can be a challenge just to keep up, let alone hold down a part-time job. These suggestions for handling the work-school balance can help:

- **The ideal scenario is to work through school breaks.** This means work over the summer months, the December holiday break, and the spring hiatus, allowing you to make some extra money throughout the year, while focusing on your studies for the months that classes and exams are in session. If you work full-time for the 16 weeks of summer, earning $12 per hour, 37.5 hours per week, that will earn you $7,200 to put toward tuition and spending money (and you may still get long weekends to enjoy the sun!).

- **If you must take a part-time job while classes are in session,** look at your class schedule and realistically assess your time demands to prepare for classes, assignments, and projects. Have a schedule of your availability prepared before you go job hunting and stick to it.

- **Campuses hire many students and are generally more understanding of the time demands than off-campus employers.** These venues tend to hire lots of students working fewer hours, rather than fewer students with lots of hours, meaning that there is more flexibility for you when you need to focus on assignments and exams.

- **Find a job that provides you with helpful benefits.** Free coffee and free WiFi come to mind. Working at a restaurant means staff meals, so your mother won't have to worry that you're eating at least once a day. Beware of working at a clothing boutique, though—if it's a good one, you just might end up owing more than you earn!

- **If you must work full-time, consider a part-time education.** That said, unless you're doing a post-grad degree well after your university years (and even then), it is very hard to do both well, and you might end up performing your studies at a mediocre level, which is a waste of the money you are working to earn—and could have a negative impact on your future employment prospects.

 **HINDSIGHT**

*I got my first real part-time job at age 14, working in a restaurant. Once I entered university, I changed jobs, but always had a part-time job during school. I was a good student and managed to get everything done, which required organizational skills and hard work. Thinking about it now, most of the really successful people I know were good students, yes, but also worked part-time from a young age, were heavily involved in sports and extracurricular activities, and basically took everything and anything on. I firmly believe that learning how to juggle priorities, stay organized, and make time for fun starts when you're at school. This is great practice for handling a busy schedule and family life later on.*

## Your First Piece of Plastic

Wow, not only are you enjoying campus life and living away from home, but here comes a very friendly bank representative offering you a credit card of your very own (with your name on it and premium shopping points to be earned!). It's this magical piece of plastic that gives you licence to take things home from the store, whether you have the current cash to pay for them or not. Brilliant!

Not really. Sorry to wake you from your dreaming, sweetheart, but you're likely going to need to pay *more* than just the cost of the item for the privilege of using that little and terribly convenient piece of plastic. Premium (payment) indeed.

Now, we're not going to advise you to shun the friendly bank representative entirely, but we are going to give you some ground rules for using that plastic to your advantage.

- **DO set up a credit card at your earliest opportunity and, hence, a credit rating.** This will be helpful when you graduate from school and apply for a car loan or mortgage.

- **DO establish a good credit rating to create a solid and reliable history of repayment.** Use your card to pay for one monthly cost that is low relative to the limit of the card; then pay the full amount off each month on or before the due date. For example, if your first credit card has a $500 limit and you use it to pay a $50 phone bill each month, immediately paying off the balance, you'll be off to a great start.

- **DON'T ever carry a balance from month to month.** The interest rates you will be charged for carrying a balance are extreme. Pay off your balance and you're essentially borrowing money for free.

- **DO keep an eye on your due date each month.** Sometimes credit-card companies change those dates on you without warning (sneaky, sneaky!) and you could make a payment late by mistake.

- **DON'T ever use more than 80 per cent of your card limit,** even if you pay it off every month. More than that and you risk inadvertently going over your limit, either through interest, fees, or charges, which will harm your credit rating.

- **DON'T use your credit card for day-to-day expenses.** It's too easy to lose track of your spending and lose control over your budget.

- **DON'T ever pay your credit card bill late,** and always carefully review your statement (erroneous charges do sometimes appear).

- **DON'T pay a big annual fee for the opportunity to earn points.** For the types of cards offered to students, the value is not usually there.

- **DO talk to your credit-card company right away if you ever have trouble** or know you are about to have trouble making your monthly payment.

- **DON'T take life insurance on your credit card.** You should have life insurance if you have debt or dependants and you may choose to use it as an investment, but you should not purchase it from your credit-card company (you can usually get a better rate elsewhere).

- **DO order a credit report and check your score** within the first 6 to 12 months of opening your first card.

- **DON'T carry your card with you if you can help it.** Keep it somewhere safe and out of temptation for impulse purchases. If you must carry it, keep a playing card covering it in your wallet; in this way, you'll be at least a little more conscious of your financial indiscretion before you grab the plastic.

- **DO challenge your friends to build rather than play with their credit.** Smart choices now can be worth a fortune later on.

## Sowing the Seeds of Your Self-Sufficiency

Probably more so than at any other time in your life, now is really all about you: your independence, and your big life choices.

It's not easy. After all, you're just starting out and not making a ton of money (yet); however, you will soon face many financial obligations, such as saving for a home, hosting a wedding, travelling, or having children. And unfortunately, all of these life events may need to be delayed depending on your debt situation.

Regardless of whether you are working or in school, if you have ever aspired to have true freedom in your life—by having the funds and financial stability that allow for choice and opportunity—now is the time to begin sowing the seeds of your self-sufficiency. Here are some rules to live by:

- **Establish a good credit rating.** In this way, when you need credit (say, to buy a car or get a small-business loan), it will be there for you.

- **Pay off your credit card and any consumer debt every month, in full and on time.** Do not let debt own you.

- **Find a little bit, even just a tiny bit, to stash away as savings that you never, *ever* touch.** (Note: room on your credit card is *not* a savings plan.) We don't need to give you a lesson on compound interest (or do we?), but a little example can't hurt. Suffice to say that if you were to put aside $50 a month for the next 40 years, you would have set aside $24,000, not including interest. If the funds earn a modest 6 per cent interest, that $24,000 will magically have multiplied to more than $100,000.

If you stash your savings in an investment that turns out to be a little more aggressive, with a 10 per cent return, you'd be looking at over $300,000. Think about it: for $50 a month, you could have a nice retirement condo in Florida—and you didn't even have to work for it!

- **Have little interest in interest.** Boyfriends and best friends may come and go, but debts—and their growing interest and economic cost—are yours to keep. Think twice about those killer heels for a big date (or worse, loaning money you really can't afford to lose). The guy they attract or the best friend who benefits may be long gone before you actually have the funds to pay for your splurge. Generosity has its limits.

- **Practise a disciplined approach to your finances, but don't lose yourself in a big, grey cloud of responsibility.** Calculate the mandatory basics, including debt payments and a bit for savings. Only access the remainder for spending.

- **Recognize that some things are actually cheaper to buy when you are young.** Life insurance and other types of insurance policies are good examples. Although you might not need the coverage at this point in your life, you can actually discount shop for later in life *right now* (and no better time than when you're young and healthy to ensure your coverage won't be denied).

- **Get ready to be your own commander in chief.** Learn to be self-sufficient and take care of yourself, no matter what comes your way. And don't fret—you need not do it alone. We encourage you to surround yourself with family, friends, and financially savvy allies and advisors to help you along your way. But above all else, you want to have earned it. There's not much else in the world more rewarding than that!

## Be the Pearl

In the end, it's about starting young: saving, investing, and planning for a future where you call the shots. You will meet many great men, but, honey, if you need to kick him to the curb later (and many of you will), you need to be able to bounce back. And as for those little splurges, yes, you deserve them. But if you want the shopping spree to continue, you better start shopping at the bank for the best interest rates. (Yep, that compound interest thing again. It will rock your financial world . . . if you start young.)

It's time to step up, girl. You alone have the power to guide your wealth creation and wealth management. And guess what? The world really is your oyster. You, darling, just happen to be the lovely pearl. (Oh, you *knew* it all along!)

# 2

## Love, Relationships, and Money

### *Finance and Relationships*

### When Finances and Relationships Mix

Moolah. Dosh. Dinero. Scratch. Dough. Dead presidents. Call it what
you will, it's the bling that often creates the most friction for couples.

Indeed, nowhere do your innermost fears become more revealed,
more potent, and more potentially explosive than when you start
mixing your money with the people you love. It is incredibly difficult
not to become judgmental and defensive when your darling starts
costing you money or questioning your choices. ("You want to spend
*how* much, on *that?*")

If you lived an entirely solitary life with no one to answer to, you
might never face conflicts over money (cats are resolutely accepting
of such matters). But really, what fun is that?

Inevitably, a handsome stranger will change your life, and love—
in all its many splendoured glory—complicates things. Of course, you
want to be responsible, generous, and open-minded; we just don't
want you to lose sight of your own needs and allow yourself to get
bowled over by someone else's interests, which is all too easy to do
with people we love.

In this chapter, we are going to look at one of the most important relationships in your life (think of that person who makes you swoon, or at least did long ago) and how to navigate it, for better or for worse, while protecting yourself *and* your money. So let's get started.

## A Bag Lady's Baggage

Nearly half of women fear becoming a "bag lady" at some point in their lives.[1] Gloria Steinem, Lily Tomlin, and Katie Couric are just a few wealthy, successful women who have admitted to the common phobia of ending up alone and living on the streets. We understand this not-so-uncommon fear completely, as the fear of loss can be very powerful.

On the other hand, too many women just can't shake the Cinderella fantasy that a charming prince is going to come along and whisk them away from a life of drudgery and rags to a kingdom of eternal riches and happiness ever after.

We're here to shake it for you. No fancy gown, no gilded pumpkin chariot, and certainly no shallow royal with a shoe fetish is going to magically show up and make your dreams come true. (Kate Middleton's nabbing of a prince was no accident. She *worked* that angle!)

As for ending up on the street begging for change, we are here to assure you that the chances of that are slimmer than a Russian model at New York's Fashion Week. However, the best way to quell your fears and reduce the odds to zero is to be fully in control of your finances and put some planning in place to handle any setbacks that life may throw at you (and believe us, they will come).

So, dig way down within your heart, reach under your soul, and peer into the darkest corners of your gut instincts. There, you will find

---

[1] Mark A. Zesbauch, Lisa Resnick, and Ken Dychtwald, *The Allianz Women, Money, and Power Study*, Allianz Life Insurance Company of North America, August 2006, https://www.allianzlife .com/womenmoneypower/main3_5.html

the black box that contains all the mysteries of your secretly coded insecurities, phobias, and probably a few irrational notions about what money means to you and what it represents in your life. Be honest with yourself, but more importantly be kind and forgiving to yourself. We all come with baggage, and we're not talking the Louis Vuitton kind.

## Your Childhood Comes Back to Haunt You

Life's baggage starts with childhood. Your personal attitudes toward money are reflected in the way you choose to spend, save, share, and earn it. And like much in life, these attitudes can stem from your earliest experiences with money and how your family's finances emotionally affected you as a child. The way you value money today is rooted deep inside of you and may not be apparent without a bit of soul-searching. So, let's dust off the Ouija board, crystal ball, or whatever you've got and have a closer look.

- **Shopaholics Are Us (not so anonymous, are you!)**

  Do you find that no matter how much cash you earn, your spending rushes to outstrip the supply? Though you might think you're merely a shopping addict, perhaps you have deeper issues with wealth and are covertly seeking to rid yourself of it at every opportunity. (Could you actually be throwing money away on purpose? Hmmm.)

- **Splurge Out, Sister**

  Perhaps financial stress was so much a part of your early life that you find yourself splurging out with everything you have because, on some level of your psyche, financial instability is normal. Not to get too self-helpish on you, but subconsciously, we all find comfort in familiarity, no matter how dysfunctional.

- ### Scrooge Is My Role Model

  At the other extreme, do you find it physically uncomfortable to spend money on yourself, whether it's for a much-deserved vacation or even a nice dinner out? Before you let anyone accuse you of being cheap, consider that, maybe, you have deep-seated insecurities about feeling worthy enough of such extravagances. Or perhaps you are paralyzed by the fear of never having enough, especially if you have a brood of little ones to look after (everything changes when it's not all about you anymore, doesn't it?).

## The Takeaway

All kinds of things could be influencing your relationship with money, before you even start trying to shake up your financial path. Who knew you could get so mixed up without even spending a single cent? With this in mind, before you even consider how money impacts your relationships with others, spend some time trying to understand how money impacts *you*.

## The Emergency Reserve (a.k.a. "Bag-Lady-Avoidance Policy")

As we've seen, never mind your relationship with others, *your* relationship with money is a very complicated thing. Crises would be so much more manageable if only we could see them coming!

Unfortunately, the best we can do is to be prepared. With that said, here is a list of things you can do right now to make sure that if disaster happens, you won't be wiped out:

- ### Let's pretend

  Imagining that things are going wrong from time to time is the first step to preparing yourself for an emergency. Might just be enough to keep you from steering all your extra cash toward yet another fabulous (but unnecessary) wardrobe acquisition.

- **Credit availability (just in case!)**

  Make sure you have access to cheap credit, such as a home equity line of credit or an all-in-one account that gives you the means to deal with temporary bumps in the road.

- **Always save (make it your mantra)**

  Stop saving every month when you stop breathing. Waiting to save until you have extra money is a recipe for disaster. With a cushion of savings in place, you can afford to think clearly and calmly in the face of a crisis (like a messy breakup). A healthy savings account gives you options and opportunities.

- **Apply the 80/10/10 rule**

  With every paycheque, spend like you only earn 80 per cent of what you really do. Borrow like you only earn 80 per cent, buy a car like you only earn 80 per cent, and so on. Meanwhile, put 10 per cent into long-term savings such as retirement plans, and 10 per cent into short-term savings for emergencies.

- **A credit card is not a savings plan**

  Stash away cash for emergencies, while paying down debt. This is not an either/or proposition. Clearing a few thousand off your credit card will feel great, until you suddenly have an emergency requiring you to rack it back up. Short-term savings accounts give you somewhere else to turn, other than high-interest plastic.

## Financial Keys to Your Key Relationship

Now that you've begun to think about your own relationship with money, we'll turn our attention to another key relationship—the one with your romantic partner. Let's look at the various phases of relationship bliss and the factors you need to consider to protect your wallet, along with your heart.

## The Dos and Don'ts of Financially Respectable Dating

First dates, first kisses, the first blush of romance . . . it's all so exciting. If you're like many of us, by the third great date, you're already imagining a home together and scribbling your name combined with his. (Funny how "Mrs. Bletch" suddenly sounds so lovely . . .)

We're not going to suggest that you slow things down—who are we to judge—but here are a few tips for dating in a financially respectable way. While these may seem obvious, trust us that not all girls know these unwritten rules.

- **DO let him pick up the tab if he invited you out and he makes the offer to pay.** Thank him sweetly of course.
- **DON'T leave the house without cab fare home and the means to pay your way,** in case he doesn't offer to pay or assumes you'll split the bill. It does happen . . . more often than you might like.
- **DO be prepared to pay in full if you invited him out.** C'mon, ladies are popping the question these days; why not spring for a date!
- **DO offer to pay your share** if it's not clear who initiated the date or if you don't intend to see him again (it's the gracious thing to do).
- **DON'T unleash your debt baggage on him on the first date.** Tales of growing credit-card debt and massive student loans need to come out at some point, but not on the first date, three empty martini glasses in.
- **DO ante up if he's picking up the full cost of your dates every time.** Offer to buy the popcorn when he pays for the movie or the ice cream when you go to a ball game.

- **DO pick up the full tab now and then if you're seeing him frequently.** It's pretty dated to assume that because he's the man, he earns more than you or has the means to pick up the tab every time. And even if he does, it's only good manners to demonstrate you're not expecting him to finance your fun (and that you can make your own way, of course—a highly attractive quality).

- **DON'T end up paying for all the costs of dating.** Patterns tend to repeat themselves. If he wants to see you, he needs to have some skin in the game too. Lazy and freeloading begets lazy and freeloading. 'Nuff said.

- **DON'T consider the cost of your outfit, pedicure, and blow-out as your financial contribution to the date.** He has no idea (and we mean *no idea*) how much it costs you to look good and trust us, it's better that way.

## The Financially Responsible Guide to Shacking Up

There was a time when a woman wouldn't dream of setting up a home with a man until he had sworn in front of God, his country, your friends and family, and a couple of his ex-girlfriends, to be with you forever, for better or for worse. Today, not so much. Having witnessed too many marriages take a turn for the worse, a growing number of couples find themselves more comfortable with other, less-institutional forms of commitment, such as moving in together, adopting pets together, having babies together, signing rental leases together, or investing in real estate together (there must be a relationship in there somewhere).

On the other hand, you and your beau may very well be planning to tie the knot, and have moved in together as a precursor to "putting a ring on it." Whatever your motivation, here is a checklist of things to keep in mind when you decide to hold off taking the plunge, yet agree to share a plunger:

- **Look at your tax situation**

  In many jurisdictions, if you live together for a calendar year, you can file taxes together as a common-law couple and take advantage of certain tax credits. Tell your honey that with the money he saves in taxes, he can buy you a very nice diamond ring! (Don't mean to be your mother, just saying.)

- **Cautiously co-sign**

  Be very aware that any joint debt you incur together (such as a mortgage, car payments, or any loan you co-sign) is not actually a 50/50 responsibility, despite how you split the payments. In the eyes of the law, each of you is on the hook 100/100. Same goes for any rental or lease agreements. If you sign it, and he takes off, it's all yours. What would you do if you had to suddenly find the wherewithal to make the full-on payments for the duration of the loan? Think about it: from a financial perspective, buying a house together is a commitment no less weighty than entering into a marriage.

- **Sign a cohabitation agreement**

  You might think it's obvious that if things don't work out, you will keep the apartment, he will get the ugly chair, and you will share custody of the puppy. But when emotions run high, you might be surprised that what seems fair to you is a far cry from what he thinks is fair. Things can get nasty quickly, especially if one of you earns far more than the other, or if the breakup is not exactly a mutual decision (and c'mon . . . is it ever *really* mutual?).

  Think of it this way: you have to draft a list of your stuff for the movers anyway. So go the extra step and make a cohabitation agreement that tracks what originally belonged to you and who gets what stuff in the event you part ways. Sign it, date it, throw it in your safe deposit box, and live your life. You may never need that list, but at least it's there if you do.

- **Keep a backup plan**

Naturally, you want to start sharing everything (sigh!), but, darling, do hold back a bit of your own nest egg. We're not advocating a secret slush fund here (okay, maybe a modest emergency glamour fund, just for pick-me-ups, of course), but the knowledge that you have a solid bit of savings in place can keep you from feeling overly vulnerable during times of relationship stress. And if and when you do decide to tie the knot, you'll have a pool of funds ready for a rocking girls' weekend to celebrate, well, your rock.

- **Know the rules of common-law**

Blame it on hormones, mid-life crises, job transfers, or wandering eyes, but the trouble always starts when one partner decides that the status quo is no longer good enough. One day, one of you wakes up and wants more, maybe marriage, children, a new house, and the other person simply doesn't buy into the dream (maybe they just roll over and go back to sleep).

Sad to say it, but statistics tell us that common-law couples are at least two times *more* likely to break up than married couples.[2] While it's complicated enough to undo a marriage contract through separation agreements and divorce settlements, breaking things off when there is no legal arrangement can be equally painful and fraught with difficulties.

Do be aware that jurisdictions define common-law arrangements differently and the legal treatment of a split is

---

[2] Statistics Canada, "The Daily," 11 July 2002, http://www.statcan.gc.ca/daily-quotidien/020711/dq020711a-eng.htm

regarded differently as well. This can affect whether or not you can claim spousal support or whether or not you have a right to split the assets.

In most cases, short-term common-law couples (typically three years or less of cohabitation; less if the couple parents a child together) do not have the same claim to financial or property division as divorcing couples. If you are dragged into a courtroom, the judge will likely consider what each of you brought into the relationship (thank goodness for that list!) and what you've jointly acquired. On the other hand, you may assume (and be relieved) that you *won't* have to deal with splitting assets upon a common-law separation, but think about it carefully. If you've been living together longer than the specified number of years, upon separation and for legal purposes pertaining to the division of assets, you might as well have just gotten married!

One thing to note is that, when a married couple divorces, the family home is considered to be a joint asset to be split fairly. In a common-law relationship, however, the court is generally more likely to consider who originally paid for the home. At any rate, know the rules in your area and plan accordingly. It most often depends on the number of years you spent living together.

---

 **GOLDEN RULE: PUT IT IN WRITING**

Documentation is critical. Never assume that you'll both remember what was yours and what was his and what you agreed to share. Memories have a funny way of drifting when the terms of the relationship change.

*(continued)*

Drafting a cohabitation agreement that lists the assets and debts that each partner brings into the relationship definitely does not feel romantic. However, a bit of awkwardness now (when things are rosy) can make a big difference if the unimaginable happens and the two of you end up parting ways. In the best-case scenario, you will have the basis of a financial plan for marriage. If the worst occurs, you will be grateful for a document that provides clarity in what will surely be an emotionally charged situation.

 **A LAWYER'S TAKE ON COHABITATION AGREEMENTS**

Cohabitation agreements are important considerations for couples living together in a conjugal relationship. Each province or state has separate legislation, but typically, after a certain number of years of living together in a conjugal relationship (in most cases, three years, or one year if they have a child together), common-law couples are covered to some degree under the legislation.

Many couples who decide to simply live together without being married fail to recognize that after a certain number of years, the law will dictate how their assets will be treated upon a breakdown of the relationship. Couples need to be aware of this so that they can properly protect themselves, because once the clock strikes that specified number of years (three years, for example), unless they voluntarily choose to enter into a formal agreement opting *out* of the legislation, they are within the ambit of it.

Always consult with your own lawyer or legal counsel to determine the cohabitation laws that may apply to you in your province, territory, or state. Being armed with information is, shall we say, golden.

## Estate Planning

In the event that you suddenly perish (for those not signed onto the immortality plan), you probably wouldn't want the government to decide how your estate will be divided, so make sure you have a legal and valid will in place for yourself and your common-law sweetie and file them in a secure place, along with financial account information and passwords.

You should know that estate plans and cohabitation agreements for common-law and same-sex couples may include eligibility for future pension benefits (something that is automatically considered in divorce settlements). Be very clear about designating beneficiaries of your insurance policies, pension plans, and any investment vehicles that allow such designations. This is especially important if you have kiddies involved.

Consider these additional situations:

- **Same-sex couples**

  Updating wills and estate plans is critical for partners in a same-sex union. Depending where you live, laws vary on how same-sex unions are treated, as well as how the estates of common-law couples are treated. The more you can do to make your last wishes legally binding, the better.

- **What about mom's boyfriend?**

  Keep in mind that aging parents often find companions in their later years (and good for them!). If your mother dies without a will or written agreement, her live-in partner could have a legitimate claim on her estate. If she does have a will and has purposefully not included her partner in it, he will have the right to contest it. A proactive legal agreement with regard to each person's estate can save a lot of family heartache. This can be arranged even if they are already living together common law, so long as they each have their own legal representation and have not been coerced into signing.

**HINDSIGHT**

*My client's common-law husband died last year in a motorcycle acci-dent. He was only 48. The couple had been together for over 20 years, and they had three children together. Unfortunately, the man died without a will. When it came to settling his estate, his common-law wife had little say in the matter—she stood third in line as an inheritor, behind his family and the government.*

## So You've Decided to Put a Ring on It

Congratulations! If you've found that lucky guy who makes you laugh (and doesn't mind that you snort while doing so), loves his job (and he's an *actuary!*), knows his way around a corkscrew, and (most importantly) recognizes you for the super-sexy rock-star goddess you know you are, then why wouldn't you want to get a ring on *his* finger? You want to make it official, share your lives together in every way, and what does that start with? Oh, yes, money.

## The Big Event: Who Pays?

These days, who pays for the wedding is anything but straightforward. Traditionally, of course, the bride's family paid for the whole shebang, with the groom's family covering the rehearsal dinner and possibly picking up the bar tab at the wedding reception.

But couples these days are likely to get married after many years out of the "nest" and have earned their own income for a significant period of time. They are used to making their own spending deci-sions and are not keen to have Mom and Dad organize their wedding (second cousin Joe, his wife Louise, and their three noisy children can stay at home, thank you very much).

Today, it is common for parents to make contributions to their kids' weddings, while couples pay the balance of the costs themselves. Most brides and grooms feel this gives them more freedom to make their own choices for venues and catering, and prevents their folks from inviting all their bridge club, golf club, and fitness-group buddies, whom the couple has never even met. Tell your folks they can relax and enjoy being *your guests*.

Of course, this means you've got to get busy and start saving for the big day (if you haven't already been doing so!). For the betrothed couple, setting up a joint savings account where you both contribute regular sums toward the wedding nest egg can be your first step toward a lifetime of financial togetherness.

## The Takeaway

The far-and-away best way to pay for a wedding is with cash. You'd be amazed at how much better you can negotiate rates on everything from the venue to the band when you've got cash in hand. Using your credit card can be a smart way to accumulate honeymoon air miles, *only if* you are able to pay off the balance with your wedding savings. (Who wants to begin a new life with a great big interest-bearing load of debt?) If you find you must carry over some costs, rather than getting stuck with high credit-card rates, look for a line of credit that offers a much lower interest rate so you can pay it off quickly (as in, those lovely fat envelopes tucked in among your wedding gifts!).

## Secrets of a Smart Pre-nuptial Agreement

We've already been clear on our position on the cohabitation agreement once you and your beloved move in together. Surely, you are expecting us to stand firm on the position of getting a pre-nup as well, right? Not so fast.

**LIFE LESSON: BEWARE OF THE DESTINATION WEDDING**

Tropical islands and medieval castles may beckon, but you might want to make doubly sure that your ceremony stands up at home. Jerry Hall and Mick Jagger were oh-so-romantically married in Bali. When Jerry kicked Mick to the curb in 1999 (upon learning he had fathered another woman's child), Mick managed to get a legal annulment, declaring that their marriage never existed. Jerry received several million dollars, but this was a fraction of what she would have received in a divorce settlement.

Whether or not you and your betrothed need a pre-nuptial agreement really depends on what you are each bringing into the marriage, in terms of things like assets or inheritances. If his biggest concern at this point is never losing the foosball table, and your most coveted asset is your grandmother's pearl necklace, then a signed cohabitation agreement will probably suffice and there's no need to call in the lawyers for a pre-nup.

On the other hand, if one of you has inherited a family cottage or has been compensated with a significant amount of lucrative stock options over the years, or if either of you has children and you want to be clear about inheritance issues, then a pre-nup is a wise move.

The primary purpose of a pre-nuptial agreement is to clarify the ownership of assets before you enter into the marriage contract. That is, an agreement that dictates how each person's individual assets acquired prior to the marriage are to be treated in the event of marital breakdown. Even if that's all the pre-nup includes, it will help a judge or arbitration lawyer to sort things out more smoothly—and less expensively for you—*just in case* things go sideways.

A pre-nup can also be used to limit the type of property division and financial support provided to the ex-spouse in case of a split. This is typically used in cases where one partner is the clear breadwinner or comes into the marriage with many more assets than the other partner.

But let's be clear: the goal of a pre-nup should never be "Your life will be a fairytale as long as we're together, but if I decide to move on, you must go back to where you came from." This creates an uncomfortable balance of power that has the potential to seep into resentment and control issues.

A good pre-nup protects the wealthier partner from losing assets that he or she earned or inherited before the marriage, while also protecting the dependent spouse from feeling overly vulnerable and fearful of instability, should the wealthier spouse leave and take their lifestyle along with him—or her. It also can be used to set guidelines in terms of how property obtained during the marriage would be distributed should the union not be successful.

While these agreements are important in all circumstances, they are particularly important in second marriages when there are children from previous marriages. So, if you've got little ones and are back on the dating scene, think long and hard about marrying again without ensuring the legacy you're building for your children stays that way . . . for your children.

Of course, pre-nups are often famously challenged when it comes to enforcement; however, a pre-nup should still be taken seriously, and not treated as something that will be overturned at some point in the future. In order to be a legally binding agreement, both parties must willingly sign it, with full financial disclosure and the opportunity for each partner to have it reviewed by independent legal counsel. (Get your own lawyer, girl!)

And remember, a document that is hastily produced and signed on the eve of a wedding is probably not worth the cocktail napkin it was scrawled upon (just ask Steven Spielberg).

**HINDSIGHT**

*This is why you need a pre-nup: My client bought a home as a single woman with $500,000 she inherited from her parents. She later fell in love, married, and her new husband moved into the home she had purchased. The marriage was okay at first, then headed into a steady decline. After five years, she called it quits. In the divorce, her husband was awarded 50 per cent of the family home, or $250,000, even though he did not contribute to any part of it. A fair and reasonable person might have waived this right, but if he were that reasonable, she probably would not have wanted to divorce him in the first place.*

## Talking the Talk for Long-Term Bliss

Finding the right partner really can change your world and your outlook. This is a great thing! The key is to not lose yourself and your values in the process and to keep your head on straight, while giving your heart.

The best advice we ever got is boring, but true: communication, communication, communication. Being able to talk openly and comfortably to one another about difficult or decidedly un-fun things is a rare skill. Foster, nurture, and practise this important skill.

With that said, here are some tips for opening up the discussions around household finances with your sweetie.

- **Who's the spender and who's the saver?**

  When a relationship becomes a household, it's helpful to recognize that each of you has your own particular strengths and weaknesses. Rather than trying to change one another, harmonious living can be achieved by complementing one another's strengths.

  So, if one of you tends to be good at savings and investments, while the other is a whiz at knowing how to shop for the best deals, go with it! Hold monthly "meetings" over a cup of coffee or a great bottle of wine to share the results of what each partner has researched and accomplished. Both partners need to understand where the household money is saved and how it gets spent; a lot of valuable information can be gained from this type of debriefing. By sharing your research and recommendations, you can make happier decisions together. Even better, no one person ends up feeling stuck shouldering all the financial responsibility, thereby reducing feelings of stress and resentment.

- **Broaching the breadwinner talk**

  When one person in a relationship earns a significantly higher income than the other (or perhaps is the only one generating an income outside of the home), it can lead to feelings of inequality that seep into other areas of the relationship. Make a point of discussing the matter openly, be supportive of the long-term career goals of each partner, and regularly recognize the give and take that each partner contributes to the relationship. A partner who stays home to raise children, for example, plays a very valuable role in the family unit, not only in terms of nurturing the next generation, but also in terms of managing the household and providing the opportunity for the other partner to be even more successful in their career.

  Do what you can to head troubles off at the pass. Protect the breadwinning partner with adequate life insurance to ensure that mortgages and debts will be covered in the event of a crisis. And definitely consider life insurance for the stay-at-home or lower-income spouse as well. There is tremendous value in being a caregiver/chef/party planner/house manager all rolled into one. Try outsourcing it (or doing it yourself, partner) and see what it costs.

  A joint deposit account that both partners can pay into and track bill payments from creates a neutral territory for taking care of household expenses. Maintaining separate accounts for paycheques and disposable income ensures a continued sense of personal autonomy, as well as allowing for secret purchases of surprise gifts for one another (or, ahem, oneself)—always appreciated!

- **The pot of gold**

Setting a goal together, working toward it, and achieving it together has a bonding effect like no other. Whether big (like getting married) or small (like running a 10K), when you set out to do something together, you are reinforcing the feeling of acting as a team.

It's remarkable how many couples do not have long-term goals. Or if they do have such goals, they don't discuss them. Living in the present is a wonderful way to live, but you also need to make sure that your day-to-day actions are not in contravention with your big-audacious-dream goal, whether that means early retirement, buying a beach house in Spain, or chucking your day job and becoming an artist or musician. Take time to frequently check in with your partner to keep your goals fresh. Ensure that your monthly spending and investing decisions are working in alignment with your long-term plan, and that each of you is contributing his or her share. You will feel more like equal partners moving forward together when you both are on the same page and have some "skin in the game."

- **His debt, her debt—OUR debt**

If you've tried to avoid the discussion, we totally understand. It's not easy to fess up to debt loads, whether it's overhanging student loans or a credit card that tends to jump out of your wallet and run wild through department stores. When you love someone, you've got to trust him or her to love you, despite your financial weaknesses or indiscretions (like the fact that you have a closet full of yoga pants, but have never been to a yoga class . . . semantics, right?). Yes, with secrets come feelings of shame, so shine a light on those dark corners of debt, honey!

Often, the sense of being on a team (it's no longer just you anymore!) makes people feel more accountable and responsible with their own money and helps them to manage their debt more appropriately. And don't forget, once you're married, his debt becomes *our* debt, so know what you're getting yourself into—both before the marriage and during it.

- **Those taxing taxes**

  While some people believe that joint-filing a tax return is optional, in fact, you are obligated to file according to your true status, whether it's single, married, or common-law. In many jurisdictions, common-law and married couples enjoy equal benefits, whether they are same sex or opposite sex. With careful tax planning and a trusted advisor, the gains from joint tax filing should outweigh any disadvantages, so make sure you are getting good professional advice in this area.

  For example, you may be able to split income, open spousal retirement plans, transfer investments without triggering capital gains, claim a spousal tax credit, and transfer credits to one another in order to lower your overall income tax situation.

- **Will you be my emergency contact?**

  When you spend every waking moment together with someone, at some point you need to ask yourself, what would happen if the worst happened? Are you each other's emergency contact? Do you each have a will and know where they are filed? Who will be the executor of your will? Who is the beneficiary of your life insurance or other investments?

  Once you get married or decide to live common-law, it's critical to update and formalize these matters. In the meantime, however, you should know what to expect in the case of an emergency and be clear in terms of on whom you can depend.

## Checklist for a Golden Girl's Financial Sanity and Security

Meetings with your honey don't need to be boring! Make these "must-do" conversations fun by opening up a bottle of wine, ordering in some gourmet pizza, and putting on your favourite music. (If that doesn't intrigue him enough to turn off the game, suggest that you watch a chick flick. Works like a *charm*.) Here's what you need to talk about and when:

1. **Monthly meeting to review the key happenings**
   - Things to know/ask/discuss:
     - ✓ How much income did we bring in?
     - ✓ Are all the household bill payments covered?
     - ✓ What major or surprise expenses did we have?
     - ✓ What school expenses did we have?
     - ✓ How much did we spend on groceries, eating out, gifts, movies, or other discretionary purchases?
     - ✓ Did we put money into savings?
     - ✓ Did we pay off the credit cards?
     - ✓ How much have we accumulated toward our goals?
     - ✓ What major expenditures are coming up?
     - ✓ Did we spend more than we earned this month?

2. **Quarterly meeting to review the family's investment portfolio**
   - Things to know/ask/discuss:
     - ✓ How much do we have invested?
     - ✓ Which financial institutions hold our assets and our debts?
     - ✓ Who are our key contacts there?
     - ✓ Where do we keep the account statements filed?

✓ What is the long-term goal for each of these investments?

✓ Should we make any changes to our contributions?

✓ How much are we paying in investment fees?

✓ Is our advisor meeting our needs to our satisfaction?

### 3. Annual weekend to go through taxes

- Things to know/ask/discuss:

  ✓ How much income are we reporting?

  ✓ Who is reporting which deductions?

  ✓ How much do we owe/will we receive as a refund?

  ✓ Are there any other possible deductions we can find?

  ✓ Are we up to date in all of our tax and related filings?

  ✓ Who is keeping track of our receipts and supporting information?

  ✓ Where do we keep our tax history and past years' returns?

  ✓ How much are we paying the tax preparer?

  ✓ Has his or her contact information changed?

### 4. Annual chat to review the insurance policies and estate plans

- Things to know/ask/discuss:

  ✓ Are the insurance premiums up to date?

  ✓ Do we still have enough coverage?

  ✓ Do we need to update our wills or insurance coverage to reflect any changes we made this year?

  ✓ Do we have beneficiaries, executors, and guardians assigned?

  ✓ Where do we keep these documents filed?

  ✓ Has our lawyer's or insurance agent's contact information changed?

Done! Now that wasn't so hard, was it? This four-fold approach is valuable in ensuring that all key financial and investing issues are addressed on a timely basis and that you and your partner are *both* in the know in terms of your finances, important information, and key contacts. Red wine and retirement planning—what's not to love?!

## Your Wifely Duties

No, not those duties! We're talking about your *financial* duties: budgeting and staying on top of the family finances. All the hard work and political efforts of Gloria Steinem and Betty Friedan throughout the 1960s and '70s mean that women today have the economic freedom and equal responsibility for the modern family's budget and household spending that is not only valued, but expected. Lucky us, it's called "the power of the purse." So step up, sister.

- **Household budgeting**

  Let's be honest: budgets rarely work. Focus instead on controlling what you can and automating the rest. For variable costs, such as groceries, dining out, travelling, books, and magazines, you can place a spending cap, either weekly or monthly. For bill payments, investments, savings plans, and debt repayment, it's better not to give yourself the option of considering or potentially missing a payment. Automate these payments from your credit card or chequing account. This approach will help you to structure your spending, make sure that the "musts" are taken care of, and set a guideline for more variable or discretionary spending.

- **A word on credit-card insurance**

  Insurance can help to cover any personal debt in an estate; however, the type of insurance sold on credit cards is very, very expensive. Better that you and your spouse have enough traditional life insurance in place to cover your debts, including credit-card debt.

If you're not sure whether or not you're paying for credit-card insurance, check your statements for charges such as "creditor balance protector" or "creditor life." Chances are you could be paying for several expensive policies that you don't even need.

---

 **GOLDEN RULE: CASH IS KING**

Ultimately, all financial planning is about cash flow. You save for retirement to create future cash flow; you buy insurance to create cash flow in the event of the death of you or your partner; and you manage tax consequences to protect today's cash flow. No matter what financial tools or planning you use, it's all about the cash flow. So when undertaking any sort of financial plan, consider the cash flow first. Will it be in or out? How much? Will you need more (or less) in the future? A professional advisor can help.

---

## Handling Your Own Savings and Investments

As your husband leafs through the Ducati motorcycle catalogue and you stress about the rising cost of tuition at Juilliard for your genius kids or grandkids, you might start to see the advantages of what many married couples today pursue—separate investment accounts.

Even if the issue is not different investment goals, many couples face the issue of simply having irreconcilable appetites for risk. Recessions and market crashes will do that to you.

Perhaps you coasted through the 1990s together, sharing a love for pita wraps, karaoke, and puffy leather couches, never imagining that you would ever find yourselves on opposite sides of the table over shares in Nortel (oops). But when the tech bubble burst in 2000 and the global financial crisis hit in 2008, countless couples watched and worried as their portfolios plummeted.

We can only imagine how many spouses who had been "in charge" of their family's investments came home to face steely eyed looks from their partners, while those unspoken, unutterable words hung in the air between them: "I told you not to invest in that stock."

So how do you avoid the blame game? Once you realize you have different levels of tolerance for risk, you can learn to respect and value those differences. After all, compatibility isn't about being the same in every aspect; it's about complementing each other's unique traits, no? Risk takers provide growth and challenge, while slow-and-steady earners provide stability. Both of which, coincidentally, have a place in any well-balanced portfolio. In simple terms, it's a hedge to risk.

From an estate-planning perspective, you may wish to keep the separate accounts joint in name (allowing for them to seamlessly pass to the surviving spouse without tax consequences), but the point of contact for managing the accounts can be different for each: one for you, one for me. With this in mind, it's important to let your advisor in on the secret that you're managing separate accounts (you know, in case you both decide to buy Nortel—double oops!). This helps manage your overall family risk and enhances returns through tax-efficient planning.

With separate investing accounts, you can sleep better at night knowing you've got a healthy chunk of the family's investments carefully tucked away in safe, conservative blue-chip investments. Your partner, in turn, can feel free to invest their portion in the more aggressive Chilean high-yield bonds (or maybe that's you, you risky little thing), without ending up throwing spaghetti at each other across the dinner table. Unless, you know, you're into that sort of thing.

**DID YOU KNOW? THE URGE TO MERGE (YOUR FINANCES)**

Should you sign up for a joint chequing account? Do you need one?

Here are the three most common ways couples handle the household finances:

- **Joint chequing account for household expenses:** Wherein each partner contributes to the account from which all major household expenses, such as mortgage payments and utility bills, are paid. Automatic withdrawals can help to avoid inevitable discussions such as, "No, you said *you* were sending in the cable-bill payment!"

- **Separate accounts and assigned expenses:** Wherein each partner has the responsibility for certain expenses. For example, the person who earns the most pays the rent, while the other partner covers utilities. No joint account necessary.

- **Joint chequing only:** Wherein partners share a single account for all their transactions. While this is a very traditional arrangement, it is increasingly rare since most people today enter a relationship with their own existing chequing accounts and automatic debits and withdrawals already established.

 **A LAWYER'S TAKE ON WILLS**

Get a will now, and develop it with a lawyer well trained in estate planning. Even if you have few assets (only debt!), you still need to consider guardians for minor children, health-care directives, powers of attorney, and how you want to gift items of sentimental value.

And remember, wills are affected by marriage and divorce, yet many people fail to recognize this. In some jurisdictions, for example,

(*continued*)

a marriage revokes a previous valid will unless, for example, the will was executed in contemplation of the marriage. Similarly, if a will provides a gift to a spouse or a common-law partner and at the time of the testator's death (the person who made the will), the spouse or partner is an ex-spouse or an ex-partner, the gift is revoked. All provinces and states have their own legislation dealing with wills, so it's important to consult with a lawyer in your area about your own particular circumstances.

## Till Divorce Do You Part

"Every divorce is like a little death," said the much-married Elizabeth Taylor. Nevertheless, the violet-eyed diva managed to rise from the ashes and fall in love again and again . . . and again.

Divorce is not only a huge emotional setback, it is often one of the largest financial setbacks a person can experience. While we previously addressed the cohabitation agreements and cautionary steps for protecting yourself in case of a breakup, there is something about the dissolution of a marriage that seems to magnify the trauma—and the legal bills.

Assets acquired during a marriage are divided, regardless of what the market is doing or whether it's a good time to sell. Households are physically split and when there are children, creating two equivalent households is obviously much more expensive than one.

Dealing with your ex can get ugly, to the point where you don't even recognize one another anymore. Experts say the most challenging part of divorce proceedings is trying to keep the blame and emotion out of the financial negotiations. When kids are involved, it can be equally tough to keep both partners focused on the stability and care of their children.

Here's how to get through the dirty deed . . . with your finances and dignity intact.

## His, Hers, and Ours: How the Finances Get Divided

When you and your spouse separate, your assets are separated. In simple terms, everything gets divided into categories: his, hers, and ours. The concept is to restore each of you to where you were financially *before* you married and split between you both whatever happened financially *while* you were married. That is, return "his" to him, "hers" to her, and split "ours" between yourselves. Once everything is given a value that you can agree on, you can then negotiate how to divide joint items.

Financial items you will want to consider in the event of a marriage breakdown include:

### 1. Property division

Who will keep the house if it is not sold? Remember, once you've agreed on what constitutes a 50/50 sharing of marital property, lump-sum payments may have to be made from one ex-spouse to another. You will want to get advice on the tax consequences (i.e., how to avoid triggering capital gains).

### 2. Registered retirement plans and pension benefits

Again, you will need to seek advice on the tax consequences of transferring these and what can be split upon marriage breakdown and how this can be done (sometimes, applications need to be made).

### 3. Child-support and spousal-support payments

Seek advice on if these will be taxable to the recipient and/or deductible to the payer.

### 4. Legal fees paid

In some cases, these are not deductible (i.e., when paid to negotiate a divorce) and in some cases, they are (i.e., when incurred to collect late support payments). As always, get proper and up-to-date legal and financial advice.

**GOLDEN RULE: THE LINE ENDS HERE**

In the event of a separation, joint lines of credit should be frozen, so that no one can continue charging expenses. Alternately, a separation agreement should specify who may use the accounts and who will be 100 per cent responsible for charges from a certain date onward.

### The "Family" Home: Which Family?

The family home falls into the "ours" category. And as many a splitting couple knows, often one wants to keep it (while kicking the other to the curb). While this may seem reasonable, especially if young children are involved, it's not always financially feasible. Consider this: if you've stayed at home to raise your children, how can you now afford a hefty mortgage payment, if your ex must now commit to his own home expenses as well? It's unfortunately not just a matter of "the kids and I deserve it," as ideal and simple as that sounds.

**So if you do want to keep the family home at all costs, ask yourself these questions:**

- Do you have enough cash or borrowing power to buy him out of his ownership in the home?

- If you buy him out, do you have enough income to carry the mortgage on your own? Too much debt is called being "cash poor" and financially, that puts you in a very vulnerable position in case of emergencies like illness or job loss.

- It is possible to use other assets rather than cash in the exchange, such as "I'll give you my pension assets for your half of the home," but that may not be a prudent trade-off for your future.

**On the emotional side of things:**

- Are you hanging on to the home because you don't want to let go of the relationship?
- Are you afraid of the impact on your children if you move them to unfamiliar surroundings or a new neighbourhood?
- Are you stressed because your home is a daily reminder of a marriage that you have outgrown?

Ultimately, you may love that home, but try to appreciate the value of a new start, new surroundings. For the sake of your future and that of your children, sometimes it's just better to hold your head high, leave the house you knew . . . and build a new home to love.

### Uncover Your Hidden Assets

Assets are what you *own* and liabilities are what you *owe*. A *net asset* is what you have left when you subtract what you owe for something from what it's worth.

**Let's look at an example as it applies to divorce and the joint home you both own:**

- If you and your ex own a $400,000 home and have a mortgage of $200,000, your joint net asset is $200,000.
- If you're mortgage-free, your joint asset is the full $400,000.
- That's great, right? Yes, until you split it down the middle and you're left with $200,000 each . . . to buy *two* homes. Not so pretty a picture.

Your *financial net worth* is the total of all assets minus all liabilities. It can be negative if you owe more than what you own. Not a good thing.

When a couple divorces (without a valid pre-nup), the net worth acquired during the union is to be divided. We repeat: the *net worth* (not ownership). Why? You may have owned the asset by yourself, but the increase in value during the marriage is considered joint (one exclusion can be inheritances). As you can see, it gets sticky pretty quickly.

**Here are some steps to uncover your assets (of the financial kind):**

1. **Start by determining the net worth that you each brought into the marriage.** That is, everything you owned or owed at the time. You may need to dig through your past and your old records.

2. **Next, find the value of everything you owned or owed separately and together at the date of separation.** Tangible assets like furniture, cars, and jewelry are worth what you can expect someone to pay for them today (which may be a lot less than what you originally paid). If one or both of you has a pension plan, owns art, antiques, or collectibles, or is a business owner, an independent valuator is strongly advised.

3. **The resulting increase in your net worth, both individually and as a couple,** from the date of marriage to the date of separation represents the net assets acquired during the marriage that may be subject to splitting.

4. **The question now is how to divvy it all up.** Get help! A financial expert can make calculations to help you understand your choices so the process is fair to both partners.

## Maybe I Can Pull a Britney and Just Annul the Marriage?

Britney Spears married her school chum Jason Alexander at 5:30 one morning in Las Vegas. After two days of marital bliss (or maybe a couple of aspirins), Brit got an annulment, reportedly claiming that she "lacked understanding of her actions to the extent that she was incapable of agreeing to the marriage."

We know what some of you are thinking, especially when contemplating a divorce: *Me too! What was I thinking? How can I annul my marriage?* Hold on, hon! An annulment is fairly rare. Essentially, it voids the marriage contract, kind of like making a legal declaration that "it never happened."

Legal annulments are usually granted under unusual circumstances, such as finding out that one's spouse is still married to someone else, or finding out the person you married is not who they claimed they were.

And consider this: legal annulments are not the same as other annulments. Following a divorce, a religious annulment is between you and your church, allowing you the freedom to marry again within your religion.

Kinda complicated, no? The lesson here: if you marry him, plan to keep him! It will save you a whole lotta financial headache and heartache down the road!

# For the Love of Those Little Cost Creatures

## *Finance and Kids*

## Kids Change Your World and Your Wallet

Ah, life will never be the same.

It's natural and it's inevitable. No matter how much or how little you have, the addition of kids creates a major diversion in your financial priorities. You brought 'em into this world, now you must pay for them, right?

Well, to a point, yes. You must shelter them, school them, clothe them, feed them, pay for their soccer and dance lessons, and care for them within an inch of your life (and as any mama knows, you'll be more than happy to do it). *But* some mamas (and you know who you are, ladies!) tend to go just a tad overboard. Think crushed velvet baby mats, pewter music boxes, and nothing but the newest and finest (hand-me-downs? not for *my* baby!). And when it comes to clothes, watch out. After all, it's oh so easy to shop for those little darlings: no need for grungy, dimly lit fitting rooms with inexperienced sales staff. See something cute for your tot . . . you just pick it up right off the rack. (It will fit them at some point, right?!)

Uh . . . wake up, mama! Unless you have oodles of discretionary income (and even then), it is reckless to let your own financial security perish while you shop for your little miss, send junior to endless sports camps and out-of-town competitions, and save solely for Janie's pricey private-school education (from ages 4 to 18, no less), never mind the post-secondary years to follow.

Why? Because it is plain irresponsible to turn your kids loose into the world without training them how to live within their means. And it's equally irresponsible to assume you'll be taken care of in your later years because you've forsaken everything now. (Reality check: your kids may not be as brilliant, motivated, and gifted as you think. Someone had to say it.)

Consider this: isn't one of the key goals of parenthood to provide your children with the tools to be self-sufficient, well-adjusted adults? Yes, the lessons you teach your kids about money, explicitly or by example, will last them a lifetime. And that's for better or for worse, honey.

With that said, in this chapter, we explore some of the important issues related to children, including how to teach them about money and the key steps to take to protect your kids. Perhaps even more importantly, this chapter includes the must-do steps to ensure your *own* financial wellness, in terms of teaching your children valuable money and finance lessons *by example*. So, let's get started.

## The Many Facets of a Mother's Love

Motherhood. The mother of all responsibilities.

Like any mothers, we love swapping tales of parenting trials and triumphs, but that's not the discussion for today. No, we are not here to talk about the excitement, the wonder, the joy . . . the headaches, the exhaustion. C'mon, you already know all that. Nor are we going to remind you of the overwhelming sense of fulfillment that nearly bursts your heart when you look into the pure and innocent eyes of that baby. For all the anxiety, worry, guilt, and inadequacy that you have unwittingly signed on for, talk to your girlfriends. Or your moms' group, your blog community, and of course, the man in your life (made you laugh!).

We do, however, wish to address one very important manifestation of motherhood: that powerful impulse to propel yourself out into the street toward a speeding car, at the very thought of that passing vehicle causing a hair to be lifted from your child's precious head. "Don't you know this is a *school zone?*!"

We get it, mama bear. The urge to protect your offspring is visceral; it overrides any worries you ever had for yourself and banishes every thought of concern for your own well-being. When you feel hungry, you rush to fix the kids lunch. When you're tired, you pretend you have all the energy in the world. When you're cold, you put sweaters on *them*. There is no *I* in *mom*. When it comes to their babies, mothers are inherently selfless creatures.

Case in point: We know women who once spent every last dime of disposable income decking themselves out in fabulous style. Women who would not leave the house unless suitably coiffed and coutured. Weekly blow-outs, manicures, and pedicures a must! Monthly highlights by the top stylist in town (home colouring kits? ick!). Designer handbags for every season and reason. And when they got pregnant, of course—designer maternity jeans all the way. You know the type.

*Now*, these women are converts to the home-colour rinse (you can barely tell the difference from the salon!). Occasionally, they will have blue glitter polish painted on their toes. They carry recyclable tote bags with extra bags tucked inside. Their uniform is black yoga pants, which they wear *everywhere*. No, these women didn't fall on hard times; they had kids. And it's their little ones who are all decked out in designer togs. Is this a good thing?

We are here to share with you three truths of motherhood that we want you to read and re-read (and read again) until you internalize them.

### The Three Truths of Motherhood

1. Take care of yourself first or you will be no good to anyone.
2. Kids don't need stuff, they need stamina.
3. Respect for the value of money is one of the best gifts you can give your child.

Now let's look at each of these in a little more detail.

## Motherhood Truth #1: Take Care of Yourself First

We know this will seem counterintuitive and, yes, you will probably feel guilty about it. But guilt is a normal condition of parenthood, so let's accept it and move forward. While you are inherently wired to take care of the needs of everyone else in your family first, you can do a much better job if you are in stable shape yourself. This means safeguarding your health, your energy, and yes, *your finances*.

One of the biggest ways women neglect themselves is by not being involved in the financial and investment decisions that affect their lifestyle and very real futures. In the course of our busy lives of trying to manage a household, family activities, and job responsibilities, a division of labour often occurs between spouses. You take care of the children's needs and he takes care of the mutual funds. Seems logical, right?

The trouble occurs when there is no collaboration or information sharing. While the majority of women are involved in the management of household expenses, very few are actually involved or *even aware* of how their spouses are investing their family savings. Does this ring a bell?

Not knowing is also a problem when it comes to keeping track of the seemingly endless—and seemingly nonsensical—financial paperwork. The truth is, simple organization (think a filing cabinet and gathering it all up) will help you sleep at night, so that if something were to happen to your spouse, you would actually know where all the important passwords, account information, insurance policies, tax returns, legal documents, and ownership papers are kept. Think about it: in the event of a crisis, the last thing you need is to dig through closets, cars, and desk drawers, frantically searching for phone numbers and unopened mail. You'll have way more important things to think about . . . like your kids' and your *emotional* well-being.

It all comes down to making yourself—and your finances—a true priority. If you're like many moms, you spend everything on clothing, food, and entertainment *for the kids* before putting even a dime into your own savings account. Credit-card bills quickly escalate when your son must have *that* skateboard and your daughter threatens to die without *those* jeans. We get it. No mother wants her child to feel left out, to feel different in any way.

But here's the thing: you're not thinking rationally and the consequences do indeed creep up on you. If you're like many of us, before you had children, you probably knew the basics (even if you didn't always follow them): pay yourself first, put the top 10 per cent of your income directly into savings, and pay off your credit card every month. Yet if you didn't adhere on occasion—say, if you splurged now and then and let the credit-card balance drift into another month—no one really got hurt, right? You'd catch up. Funny how things change. Now, you're probably asking yourself "Where did my money go?" and "Why the heck am I wearing the knockoff 'jeggings,' while my daughter has five pairs from the trendy store du jour?!" Something's gotta give. And here it is.

Now that you are supporting a family, the truth is, the rules have *not* changed. You must *still* pay yourself first, put the top 10 per cent of your income directly into savings, and pay off your credit card *every* month. In fact, it is even more essential than ever that you adhere to these rules, because there are now little lives that are counting on you to be stable, secure, and sane (okay, maybe just on the right side of crazy). Think about it for the long term. As wonderful as they are, kids have a way of creating dramatic situations and bringing sudden *expensive* experiences into your life, and you will need as much financial flexibility available as you can muster. So buck up, mama bear, get back on track, still buy your kids special things (but fewer of them), and tell Janie to get a job!

## Important Steps to Take When Having a Baby

Whether you're expecting your first, or well on your way with your fourth ("You're pregnant *again*?!"), there are some important steps you need to take to ensure your family's financial stability. It's about protecting your children (and your family) both before and after they enter this beautiful world. Here's how:

- **Get life insurance**

  Ensure that you have enough insurance to cover existing debts, replace your employment income (especially for the primary income earner), and cover any funeral expenses. It's also a good idea to have enough coverage to help the grieving family members get back on their feet after a loss.

- **Address critical illness and disability implications**

  Obtaining insurance to cover critical illness and disability to protect your family's financial wellness is a must. It is also important to protect your assets with a power of attorney over your property, as well as to protect yourself by naming someone to make decisions about your medical care should you become incapacitated.

- **Draft or update your will**

  In the event of your or your spouse's death, it is important that your family is cared for financially and that your final wishes are known. Key issues include protection of assets and how any obligations will be settled, guardianship for minor-aged children, and how your family's financial needs will be met and protected in the future.

- **Appoint someone to administer your estate**

  Referred to as an executor, estate trustee, or liquidator, this person or company is responsible for settling with creditors and distributing your assets according to the terms of your will. It's not uncommon to appoint more than one person, either to share the duties or in the event that one of the parties is unable to fulfill the obligation.

- **Appoint a guardian for your children**

  This person or persons will have the important responsibility of caring for your dependent children, typically until the age of adulthood. It is important to select guardians carefully, ensuring that they are willing and able to take on this responsibility and are able to perform the role in a manner with which you are comfortable.

- **Set up a testamentary trust within your will**

  This type of trust allows you to leave instructions in terms of how particular assets of your estate are to be managed over time. This approach holds the assets in trust for a period of time, rather than passing the assets to a beneficiary, and can be particularly useful in the case of young children.

**A LAWYER'S TAKE ON A FAMILY'S NEED FOR WILLS**

Wills are incredibly important tools for estate planning:

- **It is not only important for a woman to ensure that *her* will is current, for instance, but she also needs to ensure that her partner**—via his will and estate plan—is looking after her and the children, if any, as well.

- **With respect to wills, there are many considerations.** Not only is it important to think about who one wants to leave one's belongings and money to, but also who should be in charge as executor, who should look after minor children, and at what age should such children receive their inheritances. In some jurisdictions, guardianship clauses in wills are purely persuasive, meaning that they are not legally binding and while courts will consider them, they can also make alternate selections in the best interests of the children. In order to best protect against that fact, spouses should consider choosing in their wills the same guardians for their children so there is no need for the courts to become in charge of making such an important selection.

## Protecting the Nest

Insurance is a mother's best friend. Your home, your kids, your hubby, your health, your dog, and all the work you've put into creating a wholesome, beautiful, and happy environment for your family—*this is your whole world!* Of course, you would do anything to protect it, right? Nothing could be more logical than that. Why, then, are so many women woefully underinsured? We need to talk.

First off, if you work for a company that provides group insurance for life, disability, and critical illness, examine the options carefully. Most of these plans are sorely lacking in the event of a disaster, but do provide some protection at an economical rate and, therefore, should be a priority in terms of selecting your plan options. Your group plan could be used to provide a baseline of coverage, while "topping up" with plans you purchase personally. If you are a self-employed professional, consider individual insurance plans that emulate company benefits.

Whatever your personal circumstances are, the point is to ensure that you have all of the important bases covered. Here's a rundown of the various types of insurance protection you need in place when you have a family:

- **Life insurance for yourself**

  If you are a single mom or the family breadwinner, you need to have enough coverage to replace your income and/or pay for childcare until your kids reach age 18, pay off the mortgage on your home, cover any other debts including car loans or credit cards, and cover funeral expenses. This is a hefty list and generally represents only the minimum guidelines. Additional coverage could pay for education costs or other expenses for your family.

  If you do not work outside the home, it is still essential to at least have life insurance that would cover the cost of childcare, as well as any of your debts and funeral expenses. Alternatively, some people choose to have the proceeds of their insurance policy paid into a trust account, where the funds are managed on behalf of their children. In this way, you can set guidelines in terms of how the money is used and at what age your children would receive it.

- **Life insurance for your spouse**

  As indicated above, your spouse should have adequate coverage to also replace his income ideally until all children are 18 years of age, pay for any childcare, pay off the mortgage on the home, and cover any debts and funeral expenses. Again, this is generally considered the minimum for stability and peace of mind.

- **Disability and critical-illness insurance**

  Life insurance is one thing, but many people fear disability or disease even more (others, perhaps misguidedly, don't consider these possibilities enough). If you were to become ill or injured and could not work, can you imagine having to move from your home or cause your family to reduce all other expenses? Disability and critical-illness insurance help cover the income gap. For this type of insurance, it's best to pay the premiums yourself, either through payroll deductions or on your own, so that any benefits received come to you tax-free. If paid by your employer, the disability insurance income would typically be taxable.

- **Insurance for your kids**

  Many people choose to purchase basic-term life-insurance policies for their children, as a way of starting them out on a financial path while qualifying them for insurance coverage long before they ever need it. Insurance policies for children and teenagers are typically very inexpensive and can be approached as an investment in your child's future. Critical illness is also an option to consider for children.

- **Caring for kids with disabilities**

  Parents of special-needs children often say that their child has taught them so much about life, about what is really important and meaningful. As parents of particularly vulnerable children, one of the greatest worries is ensuring that your child will be cared for in your absence. One way to start on the path to peace of mind is to look into government-registered disability plans that offer income-based matching contributions. Often, once the beneficiary is over 18 years of age, contributions are based on their own income, rather than that of their parents, and contributions can usually continue well into middle age. Of course, policies change, so talk to a professional advisor for the most up-to-date information and to take into consideration your child's particular situation and needs.

Particularly in the case of children with disabilities, choose the trustee for your estate carefully; someone who can care for your child's special needs in the event of your death. In the case of all estate trustees, you want to name someone for whom the responsibility is not so much of a burden, as it is a privilege.

## The Takeaway

You've worked extremely hard for everything you have, and now that you're a parent, one of the best things you can do for your children is to protect their financial futures, especially if you or your spouse die or are unable to work. Kids thrive on stability. Even though life is full of unexpected twists and turns, ensure that you are at least able to give them financial stability, safety, and strength.

 **LIFE LESSON: HIS, HERS, AND THEIRS**

Blended families often suffer from the fallout caused by torn loyalties.

Although the act of remarriage is an exercise in optimism, it's worthwhile to hold onto a little pragmatism. As such, if you both have children, a pre-nuptial agreement is a good idea to protect the financial futures of everyone involved.

Above all else, recognize that blended families need blended advice. Manage expectations and recognize that your finances are simply going to get more complicated. A professional advisor can help you overcome the challenges by putting a proper estate plan in place to protect your children, even in the face of various family units. Look for advisors who specialize in working with blended families.

## Four Legal Topics to Discuss with Your Family Now

### 1. Powers of attorney

These documents provide for how one's property is to be managed in certain circumstances, mainly in the event that the person is unable for physical or mental reasons to manage his or her affairs.

Powers of attorney can take several forms. They can be operative from the moment they are executed or they can become operative upon a certain event, such as the incapacity of the person executing the document, which is called a *springing* power of attorney. If they are to become operative upon execution, it is important to note that they will only continue to be operative in the event of mental incapacity if the document specifically provides for that. This would make the power of attorney called an *enduring* power of attorney.

These documents need to be examined carefully as life unfolds because often people execute their wills and powers of attorney together. In the event of a divorce or separation, a person wants to make sure that they re-execute a power of attorney appointing another attorney if the spouse was the attorney in the previous document.

### 2. Health-care directives

Heath-care directives are important tools for everyone to consider. They are documents that allow people to appoint one or more proxies (i.e., authorities who represent you) to make decisions respecting the health care of the maker of the directive. Health-care directives can be as broad or restrictive as the person making them wishes. The bottom line is that they are documents that ensure peace of mind for the people making the directives and their family members.

### 3. Estate-planning matters

It is never too soon to start estate planning because most, if not all, estate-planning tools consider ways to minimize or defer taxes. It is very important for people to line up their professional advisors: accountants, lawyers, insurance brokers, bankers, etc. These advisors can, and should, work together.

### 4. Discretionary family trusts

Family trusts are important estate-planning tools to consider. A trust is a relationship that is created when a person (called a "settlor") transfers property to one or more persons (called "trustees") for the benefit of other persons (called "beneficiaries"). The trustees become the legal owners of the trust property; however, they are under a fiduciary duty (bound by honour and ethics) to administer the trust property in the best interests of the beneficiaries in accordance with a trust agreement, a document signed by both the settlor and the trustees.

There are two main benefits to establishing a discretionary family trust. The first is that a taxpayer can transfer his or her future income and wealth to his or her family, many or all of whom may have lower tax rates, thus resulting in savings. The second major benefit is that the $750,000 capital gains exemption (i.e., in Canada) may be multiplied by the number of family members who are beneficiaries of the trust.

As well, a taxpayer may reduce the amount of taxes payable on his or her death since transferring assets to a discretionary family trust will reduce the size of the taxpayer's overall estate.

When a trust is defined as being "discretionary," it means that the trustees alone have the discretion to determine when and which beneficiaries are to receive either the income or the capital of the trust.

It is important to note that for tax purposes, a trust is deemed to dispose all of its property every 21 years in Canada. The reason for this is to ensure that a taxpayer cannot defer capital gains indefinitely by simply transferring property to a trust with an intention to never dispose of the property.

## Motherhood Truth #2: Kids Don't Need Stuff, They Need Stamina

From the moment your pregnancy starts to show, people will start telling you what you must have for your baby. You *need* a jogging stroller. You *need* a spa baby tub. You *need* Sophie the Giraffe. It makes you wonder how generations of children ever survived without such must-have innovations!

As your children start preschool and kindergarten, they begin to articulate their own little consumerist notions. I *need* Gogo's Crazy Bones. I *need* Silly Bandz. I *need* a Nintendo DSi with a Hannah Montana skin. It's tough to keep up with the demands—and it's hard to say no. I mean c'mon, you're a mom! One truism of motherhood is that you desperately want your kids to make friends, to feel they fit in, and to not feel left out when their little friends have all these wonderful . . . things. (But do they really, *actually* have these things? Another truism of kids is that they tend to fib and exaggerate *a lot*.) Your logical side would tell you that you don't want to encourage a materialistic attitude. But your emotional side. . .

There are two important concepts that can help with this issue:

### 1. Delayed gratification

To help instill the lesson of delayed gratification, it's important to be consistent. When your child wants something—no, *needs* something—that you can plainly see is hardly essential for their continued survival, the key is to *not give in right away*.

Even if the item is inexpensive and harmless—and you will eventually buy it for them anyway—wait. Bide your time. Make them earn it either by doing small chores or by having them save up for it with their allowance and birthday money. Mark a date on the calendar and let your child cross off the days until purchasing that much-coveted item. Teach them that you can certainly have what you want in life, just not immediately upon declaring your desire. They must learn that with a little effort, they can work toward financial goals.

### 2. Opportunity costs

Your children will face many, many choices in life, so you might as well start teaching them early about how to make small decisions (chicken or cheese? green or blue?) and that every decision has a price. Learning to give up something in order to get something else is a hard lesson, when a child really just wants both (don't we all).

In harmless situations, letting a child make a choice where they *don't* end up with both options is a healthy exercise. The truth is, when they face big decisions in the future (buy that nail polish or slip it in my pocket), you may not be beside them; at least you'll know you equipped them with the power to think through choices and to understand the opportunity costs. These are important skills for both adult and child to carry out into the world.

## The Takeaway

Using this type of consistent approach can help your kids to understand the give and take in life. You might even find that once they have had a chance to put some distance between themselves and that "must-have" item, they don't even want it any more (a good lesson for all of us). Either way, they will have learned how to set and work toward a financial goal, and will have experienced how awesome it feels to accomplish what they set out to do. Yes, you have the right to be proud!

---

**WHEN CONTROL ISN'T COOL: PROVIDE THE PRIDE**

It's understandable that parents love their children and want to care for them well and provide protection from any possible harm. There is a fine line, however, between providing for your children and *over providing*, to the point that can actually hamper the ability of young people to learn and do things for themselves.

Don't let yourself fall into the unhealthy trap of providing too much and creating dependency long after your little one is no longer, well, a *little* one. Let them feel the satisfaction that comes from learning how to provide for their own needs. Pride is so much better than dependence and control; don't rob your kids of that wonderful feeling!

---

## Instill the Thrill of Saving and Investing

Here are some suggestions to truly open your child's eyes to the power of money, saving, and investing to transform their own life, their community, and the world at large. It's about stamina for their cash, not stuff.

- **Help them understand the presence that the stock market plays in their everyday lives and in everything they do.** "Yes, son, you can own a Sony PlayStation, but you can also own Sony (the corporation, a.k.a. the stock SNE)." That's a powerful message.

- **Create and track a mock portfolio.** Include a few surefire attention grabbers: Nike, Sony, Apple, Gap, Disney, Wal-Mart, McDonald's. You get the picture.

- **Make it a weekly or even daily practice to follow the big stories in the business pages with your kids,** so they'll get an idea of what makes their stocks soar and dive. You might just learn a thing or two, too!

- **For even more impact, consider giving your child a few shares** of one of those companies. (Bam, you've got them hooked!)

- **Share the lingo and the knowledge.** Bring them in to meet your financial advisor, even just to begin hearing the terminology. Better they start learning "financial speak" at age 14 (and not 40).

## Teach Them to Think Beyond Their Borders

For the forward-thinking parent who wants to open her child's eyes to the world economy, consider teaching them about and involving them in microfinance opportunities in developing countries, particularly for female entrepreneurs. By investing a relatively small amount through a microfinance organization, your family can watch your money being lent out in small amounts to deserving entrepreneurs, typically in poverty-stricken countries who would generally have little or no access to traditional forms of lending or banking.

According to PlaNet Finance, "The loans to the 66.6 million microfinance clients who are among the poorest of the poor have a direct repercussion on a total of 333 million people, or the equivalent of the populations of the U.K., France, Germany, Italy, Spain, the Netherlands, Switzerland and Norway combined."[1]

Furthermore, "It has been proven that microcredit has a positive impact on the level of profits, investments and access to

---

[1] PlaNet Finance Group, "Microfinancing, An Effective Tool for Fighting Poverty," http://www.planetfinancegroup.org/EN/microfinance.php

macroeconomic markets. On the level of households, microcredit has a positive impact on consumer spending. And on the individual level, microcredit has resulted in greater regard for spouses and children."[2]

That's one powerful message and one powerful movement for all individuals—young and old—to learn and embrace.

---

 **HINDSIGHT**

*From the time my three fashion-conscious girls were young, I taught them about budgeting around their wardrobes. We had a budget for each season (winters, with coats and boots, were the most expensive; summers, with T-shirts and shorts, were the least). I'd have them review what still fit from the last season, what they could hand down to each other, and the essential pieces they were lacking. Then, we would have a shopping expedition with their budget already set.*

*It worked well, and my friends were all very impressed. That is, until the winter that my middle daughter decided not to "waste money on boots and a coat" and walked through the snow to the school bus in shoes and a light jacket. Though she often admitted to being cold, fortunately, she didn't get seriously ill. It did make me revise the rules going forward! And here is the big lesson: don't be afraid of mistakes, whether yours or theirs. It's all part of the growing experience.*

---

## Schools of Thought on Schooling

Paying, or helping to pay for your child's post-secondary education is a challenge for most parents. Naturally, you want your child to begin

---

[2] Ibid.

their career without being burdened by debt, and therefore, have the opportunity to take jobs that they love without financial pressures. On the other hand, you do want your child to understand the value of money and the value of an education.

As with anything in life, the magic is usually in the mix. Ideally, your child could obtain scholarship funding or other grants to cover the major education-related costs and work during the summers to save up for the school term. If you can afford to make a contribution without sacrificing your own financial stability, you can help to ensure that your child comes out of university blissfully debt-free.

Here are our dos and don'ts when it comes to helping your kids pay for school:

- **DON'T forego your own retirement savings and debt obligations in order to pay for your child's education and training.** Think of taking care of your own financial health as putting the oxygen mask on yourself first, so that you can *then* assist others.

- **DON'T think of your kid's career as a brain surgeon or soccer star as your retirement plan.** Hitching your future on your child's success is unfair and adds enormous pressure, and their lives may not (likely won't) go precisely according to your plan anyhow.

- **DO find a balance where you save for yourself, even if it means that your child will have to contribute to their education** by working summer jobs or even taking a year off to accumulate savings. The bottom line is that's how life works; might as well learn the lesson young.

- **DO maximize any government-regulated education savings plans,** but be aware that some of these plans have high up-front fees and reducing or stopping payments can sometimes cause issues with how much money will be available in that account for your child. These plans can offer great benefits later on in life, but the flexibility during your child's early years might be limited.

- **DO investigate trust options for funding your child's schooling, which allows money to be sheltered and taxed in the hands of the child.** By placing the funds in trust, you are giving them to the child, but retaining control until they reach the legal adult age, when they can access the money.

- **DO keep it real.** There are many, many examples of successful people who did more than their fair share to finance the costs of their own education. This could include everything from working odd jobs, extending the length of an education program in order to be able to work more hours while in school, attending night courses, and taking a stepped approach (start with some education, work, go back to school). Where is it written that parents owe their children a full post-secondary education *for free?* Contributing to your child's education is a wonderful thing, but is a blank cheque really necessary?

## The Takeaway

The bottom line is that where there's a will, there's a way. Give your children the will to carve their own paths, on both the financial and educational fronts. As every adult knows, self-sufficiency, stamina, and self-confidence go a lot farther in this world than book smarts. (Think about who you'd rather sit next to at a dinner party: the smart, socially awkward guy; or the charming self-starter who can talk stocks, sports, or shopping. Your pick. We thought so.)

**HINDSIGHT**

*Rescuing our kids from reality by covering the full costs of their education may be one of the worst things a parent can do. In my practice, I often hear parents say, "I want to make it easier for my kids." Why? Are they broken? You don't learn much from never having to figure anything out for yourself. You can't build a muscle that never has to push against any resistance.*

*Information and education about finances is a gift to your child; paying for an education and living expenses, while your kid learns nothing about managing money, is not.*

## Motherhood Truth #3: Give Them Respect for the Value of Money

As adults, our attitudes and relationship with money began many years ago, during our first childhood experiences with the "green" stuff. Whether you're a natural saver or a spender, debt-ridden or paralyzed at the thought of carrying a credit-card balance, these inclinations are likely due to some of the early associations you had with money.

Can you remember what it felt like the first time you earned a bit of cash yourself: perhaps from making your bed, mowing the lawn, or clearing the table after dinner? Can you remember the pride you felt in collecting the coins? In keeping tabs on your piggy bank? And in making your first purchase? Or perhaps the loss or difficult-to-explain anxiety that you felt when you lost some of your money: those carefully saved coins that somehow managed to slip down the sewer grate (or were spent in a flash on some cheap toy that you soon forgot)?

Hopefully you learned something. Because now you have your own little minds to mould! Seriously, it's a great thing. You have the opportunity to teach your children about respecting and understanding the value of money without being fearful of it; how to use money as a stabilizing force in their lives, rather than a stressful one; and how to control their money, rather than letting it control them. Imagine that!

Where it begins for most children is with an allowance. Here are some things to think about . . .

## Allowance Tip Sheet

Kids value money more when it's their own. An allowance can be a great teaching tool, but you have to do it right. Consider the following tips:

- **Base your child's allowance on the expenses it will cover**

  There will be plenty of pleading and discussion in terms of the allowance amount that other children (apparently) receive. This should not be relevant in determining the amount of *your* child's allowance.

- **Set guidelines for expenses**

  Help your children to list the items that their allowance should cover. This will help them to learn how to budget and estimate costs. Don't forget to include an amount for savings, and possibly for charity.

- **Set them free**

  Give your children the freedom to spend the discretionary portion of their allowance as they wish. This will help them to understand the financial consequences of their decisions in a relatively low-risk environment. If they spend it all in a flash, so be it. It's better to learn early in life that a lack of funds is no fun at all.

- **Compensate for "real-paying" chores**

  It's best to pay your kids for chores that you otherwise would have paid someone else to do, such as clearing snow or mowing the lawn. Why? Because it is easier to understand the concept of "work" for these types of activities, as opposed to routine chores. Similarly, don't tie their allowance to chores you would expect them to do anyway. This will devalue the responsibilities of family life and create problems if (or should we perhaps say *when*) their chores aren't done.

- **No credit allowed**

  In the case of kids who overspend or cry out for an advance to make that "gotta-have" purchase, no dice! Stick to a cash-on-the-barrel rule and let the chips fall where they may. As they get older, you might consider a loan and repayment terms, but this is provided you actually follow through in demanding repayment (few of us do!).

## The Takeaway

Helping your kids to understand the concept of an allowance—how to earn, save, and ultimately, spend money—is a great opportunity to teach financial basics. Yes, *another* video game (what does he see in that?) or *another* Barbie (don't they all look the same?) is simply ridiculous but, hey, it's their money and nothing is a better teacher than suffering the consequences and regret that come from making poor choices. But it's so foolish, you think! They should know better. (All *your* little black dresses are *completely* different.)

## Age-Appropriate Money Concepts for Children

Here are some guidelines with regards to what age it's appropriate to introduce various financial concepts to your child. Of course, we recognize that *your* child may just be a genius, so keep in mind, these are only guidelines. You know best what your kids can handle and when.

### Ages 5 to 7

- ✓ counting, adding, and subtracting coins
- ✓ paying for small purchases at the coffee shop or convenience store
- ✓ earning coins for making their bed or other small chores
- ✓ saving and making a small purchase to welcome a new sibling

### Ages 8 to 12

- ✓ opening a bank account
- ✓ saving up for a reasonably attainable goal
- ✓ learning about dollars and foreign money (perhaps related to an upcoming family trip)
- ✓ earning an allowance in exchange for weekly or daily chores
- ✓ shopping under supervision with a budget and a list

### Ages 13 to 15

- ✓ understanding loans, interest, and how borrowing works
- ✓ understanding income versus expenses and how to create a budget
- ✓ understanding the real costs of car ownership
- ✓ earning money through casual jobs, such as babysitting or mowing lawns
- ✓ buying holiday gifts within a budget
- ✓ planning school items and clothes within a budget

### Ages 16 to 18

- ✓ saving for post-secondary school or training costs
- ✓ knowing how much the family house is worth (shock #1)
- ✓ knowing what the household expenses include (shock #2)
- ✓ understanding the definition of a mortgage, a mutual fund, and the stock market
- ✓ learning how to read the stock tables in the newspaper
- ✓ earning money through a part-time job
- ✓ paying their own phone bill and gas for a vehicle

**LIFE LESSON: THE GROCERY SHOP**

To start your kids on the budgeting path, let them help with items that obviously affect their daily lives, like a week's worth of groceries. Under your supervision, let them be in charge of the shopping for one week. Encourage them to start by making a list, planning around recipes, hunting for coupons, and being in charge of the shopping with cash. Let them know the "fixed" items that they *must* buy with the funds, such as vegetables, meat, bread, and milk. The items they then have the freedom to choose, or build a recipe around, are the discretionary expenditures.

This activity will help kids to:

- learn how much food costs;

- practise making multiple purchases with a fixed amount of money;

- distinguish between wants and needs;

- gain some creativity through identifying trade-offs, compromises, and identifying items that have various uses;

- feel empowered to help you find savings; and

- feel respected and trusted by their parent(s).

This real-life, first-hand exercise gives children tangible experience that you can never get across merely by discussing the concepts. So start talking and engaging your children, and start making it *real*.

## Important Lessons from a Debt Expert

**1. Shop as a family.** As mentioned above, give younger children decision-making power over a share of the grocery budget. For example, give them some discretion with their lunches (with nutritional boundaries, of course) by allowing them to choose lunch items and helping them make sure they fit within their budget. You don't have to do this every week, but a few lessons in the aisles of your local market can stick with a child for life.

2. **Do as you say.** Put the entire family on a cash allowance for discretionary spending, grown-ups included. Let your child see you spend real money; stop using the plastic for your wants. Let them watch you make choices: will it be a latte a few times a week this month or that preppy sweater you've been eyeing?

3. **Talk about salaries: theirs (in the future) and yours (in the present).** Break down the salary-sharing taboo. Your child should understand what you earn (in general), but *also* what your expenses are that allow *them* to live the life to which they've become accustomed. Next, find out what they'd like to pursue as a career, then help them research what they might expect to earn and what lifestyle they could plan around that. Not everyone needs to be a doctor or a lawyer, but they should recognize that if independent filmmaking or trekking around Europe indefinitely is their lifelong goal, that will come at a financial and lifestyle cost.

4. **Give them the facts.** Your teens should know how much you need to save for retirement, and more importantly, how long that money will last. Every year, have a family financial planning session. Furthermore, have your children sit in on a portion of your annual review with your advisor. Encourage your child to ask questions during the meeting. They need to start hearing the terminology now, when they are eager and ready to soak it up.

5. **Get them talking.** Sit down with your children and ask them how they feel about money—and then just listen. Their

responses might surprise you. What you may realize is that your children need to be armed with more than good grades when they embark into the world on their own.

6. **Give your children the gift of watching you live your financial truth.** As parents, we know (or *should* know) that life is not all about leveraging, it's not all about borrowing, and it's certainly not all about the pursuit of more. Let's teach our children to love and appreciate money, but not be ruled by it. Life has so many other lovelier things to offer . . . prove it to them.

---

 **GOLDEN RULE: THE WHOLE EQUATION**

When you talk to your kids about income, also discuss debts and expenses. If you talk to your kids about debts and expenses, discuss income. See the pattern here? In life, you don't have one without the other, so don't leave your kids with an understanding of only half the equation.

---

## Boomerang Kids

What to do if you turn out to be such a fantastic parent that your kids just won't leave? (Or they go, but keep coming back?)

It's true. Children are leaving the nest at later ages than in the past. More concerning perhaps, with higher incidences of pregnancy outside of marriage, divorce, and unemployment, more and more adult children are returning home. And they're bringing guests . . . hello Grandma and Grandpa!

They're called "boomerang kids," and once you've sent them soaring, they tend to fly right on back. Suddenly, your empty nest may start to feel just a little bit crowded. And that could mean your finances do, too.

If you feel like the front door is a revolving one, here are some tips on handling adult kids, with or without their own offspring, while in residence.

- **Charge them rent**

  That's right—put your hand out. You are not doing your *adult* children any favours by sheltering them from the realities of life. Remember: moving back home should *not* be viewed as an expense-free holiday. Even if it's not full-market value, if they earn an income, they should also be responsible for paying rent and a portion of the utility costs.

- **Forced savings**

  If they can't seem to get ahead, add a premium to their housing costs (yes, the rent), which you can then set aside and hold in trust for them until there's enough saved up for them to get their own place. Think of it this way, it's a happy little "windfall" to facilitate an earlier departure, when everyone under the roof has had enough of too much togetherness (like yesterday).

- **Home responsibilities**

  Chores are fun for all ages! Okay, not really, but they are a necessity for all ages. Adult children who live at home should be responsible for sharing home maintenance and upkeep, such as cleaning, gardening, housekeeping, repairs, painting, and trash duty.

- **Food costs**

  You can handle this issue in numerous ways, but it is recommended that your adult kid contribute to the grocery budget, as well as his or her own meal preparation. If you share meals, he or she can at least be responsible for purchasing and cooking a meal for the entire family on a weekly basis.

- **Make it official**

  To keep the details of the living arrangements clear in everyone's mind, write up an agreement that covers contributions for expenses, such as rent, food, utilities, and possibly vehicle use, as well as the household chores. You've committed to letting them stay with you for the short term; they need to commit back.

- **Exit strategy**

  Let them know that while you will always have a place for them to fall back on, you do expect them to live on their own at a certain point in time—then set that point in time. Discuss an exit strategy, set a reasonable timeline, and offer to help them with the steps necessary to get there. Calling the movers is a start.

- **Consider scaling back your residence**

  Those with (previously) empty nests often plan to sell the family home in exchange for smaller digs, or perhaps buy a condo and a small vacation property. If you are still living in the family home, perhaps with numerous bedrooms, bathrooms, and family spaces—and your adult children keep coming back—this might just be the time *for you to move*. It gets the job done.

## But What If Your Boomerang Kid Is Still Broke?

- **Don't just give them money; offer them a small loan** (*but only* if you can absolutely afford this without sacrificing your financial stability). This will help preserve your child's dignity and is fair to your other children.

- **Sweeten the deal.** The loan can be interest-free or interest-deferred, with no repayments due until your child is established. Typically, parental wills forgive such outstanding loans and reduce the borrower's bequest accordingly.

- **Get them outside help.** Arrange for them to seek advice from a financial professional to help them better understand budgeting and debt management.

## The Takeaway

Your baby will always be, well, your baby. A mother once, a mother forever, right? Yes, but with limits. You can and should be there to lend a sympathetic ear or support when needed; however, the best you can do for your children, at any age, is to keep *yourself* strong and keep them on track to being self-sufficient and confident adults.

Remember, you can borrow for their education, wedding, home, career, and family, but you can't borrow for *your* retirement. Put yourself first, mama bear, and teach those little cubs to roar.

## The Sandwich Generation

You just paid the last tuition cheque for your youngest child, financing it out of your cash flow because you weren't able to save enough for all three kids. It has been a burden, but you are finally taking a sigh of relief, which is, of course, when your mother calls. She is on a trip in France and she fell and broke her hip. You discover that she didn't purchase travel medical insurance because of the cost and now she is in a hospital and requires emergency surgery. (Or potentially more challenging, she's on her way home . . . to live with you. Say goodbye to the guest room, honey! It's now Grandma's digs.)

When this happens, you know you've entered the sandwich generation. You're caring for kids, you're caring for elderly parents, and the meagre filling in between is, well, you.

Yes, when you're caught taking care of three generations (yourself included, don't forget), getting ahead financially can feel futile. Though it might seem simplistic, open communication in these circumstances is critical. You should not treat your mother like your teenager, but be aware that, like your child, she may be facing difficult financial and emotional decisions with a lack of understanding or knowledge of their implications.

Ask lots of questions, be ready to explain financial consequences, and help out by directing your parents to trusted professionals who can give them good advice. Staying close and keeping the lines of communication open is a good way to be there without giving up everything of yourself and what you've worked so hard to build.

Remember, someone's got to care for *you* too.

.

# 4

## Building Your Dream Career

*Finance and Work*

### Getting More from What You've Got

Whether you have one job throughout your lifetime, or twenty, one fact remains: your career is the primary driver toward your financial independence and your growing knowledge base. Therefore, it is essential that you squeeze out as much benefit as you can from each and every job you will have over the course of your career, in terms of both compensation and experience. You have to work it, girl!

If you're like many of us, you put in long hours for the sake of your career—sacrificing time with your honey, workouts at the gym, family commitments, and any little bit of "me" time. But how do you keep your job from becoming "all taking and no giving"?

In this chapter, we are going to explore ways to get your job working harder for you, as well as the opportunity to utilize employment to fully develop and enhance your potential for future growth. From your benefits plan to professional development to severance pay, there are plenty of areas where you may be leaving money on the table. Time to collect, sister.

## How Can I Make My Job Work for Me?

Gossipy co-workers, grumpy bosses, evil photocopiers, or the inevitable run in your stocking: the workplace has oh so much fodder for headaches and frustration. But could that be a silver lining we see (or, wait, that's just the glare off your streaky computer screen)? Whatever it is, let's have a closer look.

For women working nine to five, eight to six, or ten to midnight, your job not only takes up a majority of your waking hours, it shapes your mind, affects your mood, and, to some extent, determines who you are in the world. It may be hard to believe (or not so hard at all), but those who are employed full-time actually spend the majority of their waking hours on the job and with co-workers, so when you spend this much of your time devoted to something (anything!), it's impossible not to be influenced by it in a very meaningful way.

It isn't just the job either; it's *how* you do the job. The quality of work you do every day has a huge impact on your self-esteem; conversely, your pride and sense of accomplishment influence your attitude toward your job. (Think about it. Was it the cockiness that made Simon Cowell famous or the fame that made Mr. Cowell cocky? It's all interrelated.) The experiences you gain and the level of success you attain will also affect your future career options. And, of course, doing a job well doesn't just apply to the high-paying "status" jobs, but to each and every job you do, no matter the title. (Want proof? Talk to Ursula Burns, the executive assistant turned CEO of Xerox, and the first African-American woman to be CEO of a Fortune 500 company. She didn't let any title stop her from climbing—not clawing—her way to the top.)

Yes, no matter the job, it's the right kind of attitude (as in, the way you carry yourself and the pride that you put into your career and your work life) that has the potential to move you forward and up the ranks. So, grab onto that ladder and start climbing!

## Someday This Job Will Make Sense

Of course, getting to the point where your job is infinitely rewarding and fulfilling usually takes time. Nearly all occupations require training and learning on the job, long hours of not-so-glamorous tasks, proving (and improving) your abilities, education, and designations— and all for what? To gradually earn positions of greater authority and autonomy, of course. Yep, it's a climb (and a grind).

According to the U.S. Bureau of Labor Statistics, wage and salary workers remain with their employers for approximately four years.[1] Spread over the 40 years of a typical working life, that translates into an average of 10 jobs throughout a person's career. Add in part-time jobs and contract positions, and you may be looking at even more.

So here's what we want you to do: think of your career as a feature-length film. It may be long, diverse, and not necessarily linear. The jobs you take, even if they're not your "dream" jobs, are like subplots of the film, each with its own purpose, storyline, and characters. (Whether yours resembles *The King's Speech* or *The Hangover* is, well, totally up to you.)

Each job will put you a little further ahead in terms of accumulating wisdom, skills, and, hopefully, money in the bank. And don't forget your supporting actors; they will play a key role in elevating (or conversely, impeding) your craft.

So, play your part with intelligence and conviction, be mindful of your supporting players, and eventually, the jobs will start to add up, larger themes will emerge, and something bigger and more meaningful will take form: your career.

---

[1] Bureau of Labor Statistics, "Employee Tenure Summary," United States Department of Labor, 14 September 2010, http://www.bls.gov/news.release/tenure.nr0.htm

**GOLDEN RULE: PAY ATTENTION**

There is no job or career path where you don't have to worry about money. There are many examples of celebrities who failed to keep an eye on their money or trusted the wrong people, and went bankrupt or faced financial crisis. So guess what? It really doesn't matter how much you earn.

As your paycheque grows, so do your responsibilities and obligations. So stop chasing unicorns (or powerful unions or status uniforms) and accept that paying attention to your money is a requirement in this life! A great job or a successful business can help make money matters a little more fun and possibly less stressful, but they never excuse the need to pay attention to your money.

## First Things First: How Do You Want to Work?

At some point during your career, you may find yourself with the option of accepting a job as a full-fledged employee of a company or as an independent contractor (essentially meaning that you are self-employed). Both options come with advantages and drawbacks. This is not a time to throw caution to the wind; take the time to understand your options and think them through.

There are many factors that are important to consider when choosing how to work. For example, if you are planning to become pregnant in the near future, you may be keen to sign up as an employee of a company to gain stability, as well as to take advantage of the maternity-leave benefits, which would not be as readily available to you as an independent contractor. On the other hand, if you prefer to do most of your work at home in your bunny slippers or on a cellphone while on the go, you may choose to work as an independent contractor and take advantage of the flexibility and work-related deductions for income tax purposes.

When evaluating your options, consider the type of student you were in your university or college days. Were you the type who preferred to study in a group and learn from an instructor? Or were you the type who actually got better grades when you skipped class, studied on your own, and set your own timetable and lesson plan? We're sure you can figure out where we're going here. If the former rings a bell, you probably thrive when surrounded by colleagues in an enriching work environment. And if the latter calls out to you, you're probably reading this at 3 a.m. after finishing up your last contract project. As with much in life, when looking toward your future, always look for hints in the past.

## Employment versus Contracting

As a general rule, employees and independent contractors are defined by the following factors:

- how much control the payer has over the worker;
- whether or not the worker supplies her own tools and equipment;
- whether the worker has the right to subcontract some or all of the work;
- the degree of financial risk taken by the worker;
- the degree of responsibility of the worker's investment and management (who is boss);
- the worker's opportunity for profit; and
- any other relevant factors, such as written contracts, documents, and the like.

## The Takeaway

Tax authorities typically have criteria that determine whether or not a person is an employee or contractor, based on some of the factors listed above. This is important to understand, particularly if you think you are an independent contractor, but end up being deemed an employee. This situation has a number of consequences, such as contractor-related expenses potentially *not* being deemed tax deductible, requiring you to make up any necessary withholdings, perhaps with interest and penalties.

Know where you stand on these tax criteria before the government comes a callin'. A tax professional can help.

---

 **GOLDEN RULE: 80 PER CENT OF NET**

When you accept a compensation offer, ask for an estimate of the amount of cash that you would receive on a net basis (i.e., after taxes and other required deductions). You might be surprised at how much *less* the net amount is (where did my money go?). This will give you a sense of what you will actually take home. If you can live comfortably on 80 per cent of the net amount, then you know there will be room to save, have money for emergencies, and invest while you pay down any debt.

---

## Signing on the Dotted Line

Landing a new job is a time to celebrate, especially when it comes with an "enhanced" paycheque! Indeed, if the pay is truly fabulous and the job tremendously exciting, it can be tempting to sign whatever offer they put in front of you (let's get this party started, right?).

Slow down. Put down the champagne bottle for just a moment and take the time to read the details. Yes, those pesky notes in fine print. In addition to the basic employment matters, such as the position and compensation specifics, employment agreements may include the following:

- **Code of conduct**

  This guideline stipulates the manner in which employees are required to behave, as well as specific actions or behaviour that will not be tolerated and can be grounds for suspension or dismissal. Be mindful that rules could apply to behaviour during both the work day, on-line (hello friends tagging you on Facebook!), and at any company-related social functions during off hours (so think twice before you reach for that third vodka-cran at the office wind-up).

- **Confidentiality provisions**

  Employees are typically required to keep any employer or client-related information confidential; this clause may remain in force even after you leave the company's employment. Always follow the rules, even during after-work dinners with co-workers. You never know who might be at the next table.

- **Non-competition clauses**

  This type of clause prohibits employees from becoming employed with the company's competitors for a period of time (sometimes several years), after ceasing to be an employee of the company and could apply whether you leave voluntarily or are dismissed.

- **Non-solicitation clauses**

  This type of clause prohibits employees from approaching the company's customers after leaving employment with the company, and may also extend to not allowing former employees to approach their former co-workers to offer them employment elsewhere. Again, this type of clause can remain in force for several years, so if your bright idea is to quit your job and take over all of those customers you have such a great relationship with, think again!

Not adhering to these provisions may not only set you back professionally and financially, it can also land you in court.

Consider this as well: typically any materials (including intellectual property) that you develop while employed are the property of the employer, not you. So, any steps to commercialize that great web program you developed and distribute it to the mass market could result in big trouble.

Similarly, even more personal intellectual property (say, the novel you've been writing and piecing together for years or a small business that you work on after hours), could be deemed to be the property of your employer. It's worth looking into seeking permission in advance, and potentially having the employer sign off on any ownership or rights to your newest venture, provided it is not deemed to be in conflict with your employment contract. When in doubt, talk to a lawyer specializing in intellectual property or employment law.

Above all else, read your employment agreement carefully and be familiar with the contents of it during the course of your employment. If you are unsure of the terms, seek out assistance from a lawyer, human-resources professional, or someone you trust who has a good level of career experience.

Once you've done that . . . have that glass of champagne. (Just not at your new desk; we're pretty sure there's a rule about that, too.)

## Best Job with Benefits

Compensation is about so much more than just the cash. Flexibility, autonomy, and a self-managed work environment can provide a level of fulfillment that cash alone cannot.

Younger employees (who never get sick and believe they will live forever—is this you?) tend to downplay the value of non-cash compensation, such as employee benefit programs. Yet for parents with growing children who need braces, professional counselling, and allergy prescriptions, a robust benefits program can be a huge incentive.

Let's take a look at some of the common types of benefits a new employee must consider when evaluating a job opportunity. (As for those "fringe benefits" such as free sandwiches during board meetings, a headset for your phone, or an office with an ocean view (ha!), we'll leave these to you to negotiate. Do us proud.)

- **Health and dental care:** These programs cover health-related expenses, including health and dental visits, paramedical services (such as therapeutic massage therapy and licensed nutritional services), prescriptions, facility-related care, and various health-related items (i.e., prescription glasses, prostheses, etc.). Coverage can vary greatly, depending on the plan, in terms of services that are covered, annual dollar limits of coverage, and employee-paid deductibles. Benefit plans can provide for single coverage (for the employee), or coverage that extends to the employee's family (i.e., spouse, dependants, etc.). There may also be various levels of coverage available at different price points, and plan costs may be paid by your employer, paid by the employee, or shared. Look at your history of claims and your personal concerns to get a sense of an appropriate level of coverage for you and your family. If you anticipate significant dental or prescription drug needs, for example, you should factor that into your choice of package.

- **Health spending accounts:** This type of program generally provides employees with a specific dollar amount per year (either a fixed amount or based on a percentage of salary) that can be spent on an employee's health-care requirements. These plans give employees added flexibility, in terms of how the funds can be allocated, so long as they are considered to be medical expenses (often, as specified by tax authorities) and can also be used to top up more traditional health-care plans.

- **Life insurance:** Comprehensive benefit plans may include life-insurance coverage of a specified minimum amount (say two times an employee's annual salary) with the option to purchase additional coverage, often at a relatively low rate. Life insurance is also an excellent benefit that can be used to cover any outstanding debts in the event of your death, as well as to provide for your family or beneficiaries. In a group plan, you don't typically have to take a medical test or otherwise qualify and the cost is usually lower than that of an individual plan.

- **Employee-assistance programs (EAP):** These plans provide confidential counselling services to employees and their families and may also include financial and legal counselling, with qualified professionals. Given that most people experience a crisis of some type during their working life (i.e., divorce, death of family members, illness, substance abuse, problems with children, legal situations, etc.), an EAP can be a valuable lifeline when you need help. Ask your EAP provider if you can choose a local service provider, as access to local professionals may be of more use in certain situations.

- **Professional development programs:** One of the benefits of being employed by a big organization is that they typically have a number of professional development programs available and will often pay for courses that are relevant to your job. Take this as an opportunity to advance your knowledge for free and learn all you can: complete a professional-designation program, improve your PowerPoint or accounting software skills, or take a conflict-resolution course (comes in handy when negotiating with your husband about dishwashing duties).

## The Takeaway

Benefit plans can amount to thousands of dollars of coverage that your employer is paying on your behalf each and every year that you are under their employment. Although this might be difficult to quantify as an employee, the message becomes evident if and when you become self-employed and have to seek out and pay for this type of coverage on your own.

Particularly in terms of health and insurance programs, the greatest value is often in *not* needing the coverage, but in knowing that it is there for you if required. Peace of mind is underrated.

---

 **GOLDEN RULE: YOUR BENEFIT YEAR**

Make sure you know whether your benefits begin and finish over the course of a calendar year, over your employer's fiscal year, or from your employment start date. If you don't know your plan year, you could miss out on valuable benefits.

For example, if your plan year starts January 1 and you have not used your $2,000 dental limit before December 31, you will lose it; however, you can plan around this so that the majority of the work you need will be covered. For example, if you have $3,000 worth of dental work to get done, schedule some procedures prior to December 31 to use up the $2,000 for that year, and have the remainder done after January 1, when a new $2,000 becomes available. You can protect your cash flow by making the most of your benefits plan.

---

## Disability and Critical-Illness Insurance: the Basics

### 1. Disability insurance

Women are statistically more likely to suffer a prolonged disability than men, so this is an important benefit to understand

and consider. If the benefit is employer paid, then the benefits are typically taxable; however, if you pay the premiums through payroll deductions, the benefits are typically tax-free. Disability coverage typically comes in two varieties: long-term disability insurance and short-term disability insurance, both of which have specific requirements in order to collect the benefits. Also, because disability plans can be expensive for companies to provide, as compared to other types of benefit plans, there may be a minimum amount of time on the job, or a "waiting period" that must occur, before new hires can be covered.

But disability coverage has limitations and doesn't cover all eventualities:

- It doesn't replace your full income; only a portion of it, which probably won't allow you to maintain savings.

- Depending on the type of coverage, you may qualify for benefits for only a limited time.

- Coverage usually stops at age 65 or retirement, whichever comes first. After you retire, you may no longer be insured.

## 2. Critical-illness insurance

This type of insurance protects you in case of a serious, life-threatening illness and typically provides a specified lump-sum payment under specified circumstances, giving you financial freedom during a time of crisis. There are various types of coverage available and it is important to read the fine print to understand the terms and conditions, as well as the particular illnesses and circumstances that are covered.

It can be a powerful addition and complement to disability insurance, in that it comes in to cover what disability insurance can't. Critical-illness insurance:

- typically provides a lump sum of tax-free money 30 days after diagnosis of any one of the major illnesses listed in the policy, such as heart attack, stroke or life-threatening cancer;

- can often go to age 100, which is important because illnesses, such as heart disease and cancer, are more likely to appear after age 65 (when disability insurance usually stops);

- benefits will allow you to pay for whatever extras you choose, such as private nursing care or housing modifications (disability insurance can then cover basic living expenses); and

- is not tied to your ability to work, though disability insurance is. You can be eligible for critical-illness coverage even if you don't work, don't have an income, and therefore aren't entitled to disability insurance. And for employed people, if after a diagnosis you return to work and therefore aren't eligible for disability benefits, you can still be entitled to the critical-illness lump sum. In many cases, you can receive both.

## Side-by-side comparison

|  | Disability insurance | Critical-illness insurance |
|---|---|---|
| **Waiting period** | Generally between 30 and 180 days | Typically 30 days |
| **Benefits** | A preset percentage of income, paid monthly, usually for a limited time | Pays a lump sum from $10,000 to $1 million (approx.) |
| **Taxation** | Benefits are taxable to employees if they are funded by their employers; tax-free if self-funded | Benefits are tax-free |
| **Coverage period** | Usually to age 65 or until retirement | Up to age 100 |

Please note that all of the above are averages, estimates, and generalities. Always speak to a licensed insurance professional to secure the most accurate information and advice for your personal needs.

**GOLDEN RULE: PAY THE PREMIUMS**

Whenever possible, pay 100 per cent of your long-term disability (LTD) and short-term disability (STD) premiums yourself. When you pay the premium, the benefit is typically not taxable. When your employer pays the premium, those benefits are typically taxable to you as income, which can result in an erosion of valuable cash when you need it most.

The premiums in most group plans for disability insurance are actually quite small, as compared to buying this type of coverage on your own, and are totally worth taking a small bite out of your current cash flow in order to protect this very valuable future cash flow, in the event of you being unable to work.

## Free Money: Pension Plans

Paycheques come and go with frightening speed. It may only be when you see the quarterly statement of your pension plan (also known as your "group savings plan")—should you be so lucky to have one—that you really start to feel that you are actually accumulating some degree of wealth. It's a great thing (talk about a sense of accomplishment!). Here are how these savings plans work.

Many companies offer retirement plans and other types of savings plans using payroll deductions to secure the same amount from you every month. This money is typically placed in a locked-in account that is held for your retirement. The real genius of this plan is when your employer provides a matching fund. In some cases, it's dollar for dollar; in others, it's a matching amount, up to a certain percentage. This is *free* money and must never be overlooked.

In most cases, if you leave the company before two years (which represents the vesting period of the plan), you get your own savings back, but not the portion that the company put aside for you. Keep this in mind if you are thinking about quitting your job after 23 months of service! By holding on for another two months, you will part on much wealthier terms (it's worth sticking it out, no?).

If you move between companies, it is sometimes possible to move your retirement plan with you, but more often than not, you need to take the *commuted value* (the lump-sum amount of money you will receive when leaving your plan early, or the present value of the future pension payment) and put it into a locked-in account. As a result, you will not be able to touch these funds until your retirement, and then, only within a range so that the payment stream lasts for your predicted lifetime (based on actuarial tables).

Group savings plans typically come in two varieties: *defined benefit* and *defined contribution*:

### 1. Defined benefit: "old school"

Defined benefit plans provide the pensioner with guaranteed income. You and your employer contribute every year, and the amount you receive in retirement is based on a formula, often related to your five years of best earnings (or typically, your last years' worked, due to seniority and inflation). The market risk is completely carried by your employer and not by you. You don't make any choices about where or how the money is invested because the end result of what you get is based on your income and years of service, rather than on an investment return.

Most of these plans began at companies decades ago under the assumption that people worked and contributed to age 65, got their pension and gold watch, and then died at age 70. During the tech boom, defined benefit savings plans were viewed as old school, but since the tech bubble burst, there has been a newfound appreciation of this approach.

Some companies, however, are crippled by their pension obligations as are taxpayers, since public-sector pensions are primarily defined benefit. The pensions are underfunded, once the lengthy retirement lives of pensioners today is considered.

The pensioner is at risk if the company goes bankrupt and cannot fulfill its pension obligations. This can also happen with governments, such as in the case of retired judges in California being subject to holds on their pensions, as the state sorts out its finances.

Criticized by some as paternalistic and by others as overly rich, this pension approach is likely to be less available in the future, so it may be worth signing up if and while you can.

### 2. Defined contribution: "modern times"

Defined contribution plans do not offer a specific income amount. Instead, you and your employer both contribute to the pension plan every year, and the amount you receive in retirement is based on whatever you have earned on the total amount contributed. In this case, the risk and reward are yours; clever investing can thus lead to improved retirement benefits. You do typically get a choice in terms of how the funds are invested, but investment selection may be limited to funds that are managed by the pension provider.

Most companies today are gravitating toward this type of pension plan. Even if the company goes bankrupt, your savings are secure because they have been accounted for all along, rather than being accrued as a future liability.

If you change jobs frequently, this plan can typically be moved to a locked-in retirement account. As with the defined benefit plan, the employer contributions only vest after a stated period of time, usually two years.

**GOLDEN RULE: TAKE THE FREE MONEY**

If you make an average salary over your working life (from age 25 to age 65) of $88,000 and refuse to participate in a group savings plan (where your employer matches up to 3 per cent of your salary), you would be giving up roughly $1,016,068. Yes, that's the power of free money, combined with compound interest. Don't pass it up.

## Stock Options: Hot or Not?

Often, when a company is trying to keep a lid on the salaries it pays out, it will offer current and potential employees stock options as part of an overall compensation structure. This approach can also act as an incentive for employees to feel a sense of ownership in their company.

A stock option gives you the right to purchase a corporation's stock at a set price, for a certain period of time, subject to certain terms and conditions, regardless of how that stock performs.

For example, if you exercise your stock options and purchase your company's stock for $50 per share, while the market price of the stock is trading for $75, congratulations, your options are "in the money" and you've just built some serious wealth! Wasn't that easy?

However, stock options can also turn out to be not exactly worth the paper they are printed on, in the event that the *exercise*, or *strike*, price (say, $100) is in excess of what the shares are actually worth at the time the options must be exercised (say, $60). In this case, the options are considered to be "out of the money," with limited incentive for the employee to pay the price to purchase the shares (unless there's some big secret you're not telling us, and that's called insider trading . . . a big no-no!). In this type of situation, stock-option plans, with all their paperwork and time and effort to administer, may be of little value (pun intended).

Stock options were once very much in vogue, especially among start-up technology companies that were short on cash to hire employees and long on expected growth potential. Many employees became dot-com millionaires in this way. Yet, when the technology sector crashed, many start-ups (and we mean *many*) failed and the employee stock options became worthless.

So, before you leap for the offer of options and start researching real estate on the French Riviera, consider the following:

- the likelihood that the stock options will ever increase in value to generate significant gains;

- how much you will have to pay for the stock options within a specified period of time, in order to participate in earnings from value appreciation;

- possible tax implications that may occur, upon receipt of the stock options, as well as when they are exercised (i.e., paid for) and sold;

- what is the liquidity of the underlying company if you exercise your options? Can these shares be sold or monetized? While this may not be an issue if purchasing shares in a publicly traded company, in many cases if you are working for a private company, you might be in a situation where you are required to hold these shares until the company itself monetizes (i.e., sells); and

- what, if any, special conditions apply to these shares when you purchase them? Read the paperwork carefully; many private-company plans have very strict conditions to hold their shares and you should be aware of these conditions (sometimes known as the "golden handcuffs").

As these factors demonstrate, being offered stock options is a good reason to seek out professional advice. The requirements and implications, particularly from tax and legal perspectives, can be complex.

## How to Ask for More: a Checklist

Salary isn't everything, though for most of us, it's high on the list. You might love your job, yet you really need more pay or benefits to feel appreciated, to feel confident that your level of compensation is sufficient to meet your needs. Sometimes the greatest job is one that you just cannot afford to keep.

While you may think that if your company could pay you more they would, did you ever think it all comes back to you; as in, *you* making the move and making the ask, rather than the other way around?

Yes, if your company values you and understands that you are contemplating leaving for greener pastures, a good employer might just surprise you. After all, hiring and training new staff members is not only expensive for employers, it is also very time-consuming. So, it might just be worth their while to keep star employees happy and promote them within the company.

Some creative solutions that you might want to discuss with your employer include:

- providing you with a bonus on a quarterly basis, rather than annually (opportunities for you to invest funds and allow compound interest to work its magic);
- giving you days off or flextime in lieu of overtime;
- restructuring your hours;
- phasing in a salary increase;
- planning for a promotion;

- finding you extra assignments for additional income (and to learn new skills); or
- boosting your benefits plan.

The important thing is to communicate honestly and directly and consider the alternatives thoughtfully. When it comes time to negotiate, make sure you've got these bases covered:

- **Speak with your boss and not with other colleagues**

  She or he will appreciate your professionalism for approaching the situation directly, rather than hearing about your concerns through the office grapevine. Plus, you're more likely to work out a customized arrangement if you keep it confidential.

- **Come prepared with a list of your achievements**

  Highlight those examples where you've gone beyond the expectations of your role. (In other words, it's not enough to say that you're broke and need new tires for your car.) You might think your boss is aware of all your hard work, but it always helps to be reminded. Just like you, a boss can be consumed with his or her own job, as well as managing other employees, so don't assume that your issues and accomplishments are top of mind.

- **Know your priorities**

  There are many factors that your boss can tinker with to adjust your role: money, time, title, recognition, administrative support, an office with a door. What are the things that motivate you and what can you live without? Think about this carefully and in a pragmatic manner. Doing so can help your boss to say yes.

- **Have a clear proposal**

  If it's a raise, have a figure in mind. If it's more benefits, be specific. If you need flextime, suggest how you will structure your day to ensure no work falls by the wayside. If it's a professional development course, demonstrate how your learning will contribute to your performance results. This approach helps you to think like a boss, utilizing a solutions-oriented approach that is a big facet of management.

- **Gather some leverage**

  Prove that what you're asking for is not unreasonable by showing what others at your level or in your field are earning. Many industry associations offer salary-survey results, and employment websites compare similar jobs and what they pay. (This may also have the ancillary benefit of helping you discover some alternative options. So, don't shoot from the hip, be in the know!)

- **Make a deal**

  If your boss isn't ready to grant your request immediately, ask for quantifiable goals; find out what you need to demonstrate or accomplish in order to get a promotion or salary increase. Establish a realistic timeline for getting these tasks done and then set a date to reconvene once the goals are met. Then ensure the goals *are* met; sooner, rather than later, if you can.

- **Put it in writing**

  After your meeting, send a thank-you e-mail summarizing your discussion and the terms to which you both agreed. And then get busy.

---

 **HINDSIGHT**

*Preparing yourself for change can lead to solutions you never imagined. I was involved in talks to change my job at one of the major banks. It was to be a lateral move, just reporting to a different department. My*

*(continued)*

*role would be new to this department and I started to get the feeling they might make me a low-ball offer ("budget cutbacks, best that we can do, yada yada"), so I called some friends who worked at competitor banks, to find out what their companies were paying for similar roles. I had no intention of leaving the company where I worked; I just wanted some facts in my back pocket for making a case to preserve my current salary.*

*In the course of making queries, one of the competitors asked if I would meet with them for an interview. Out of curiosity, I went for the interview and was surprised to be offered a great opportunity! I ended up leaving my original employer and accepted a job with the competitor, where I was given a much bigger and more exciting role—and a higher salary.*

## Investing in You: Tips for Improving Your Work Competency

It has often been said that any job worth doing is worth doing well. A way to put this philosophy into practice is to view every project you complete, or every job you hold, as an opportunity to enhance your capability—and your resumé. You know the drill: complete the task, repeat the task, master the task, own the task! Best of all, once you master a task or expand your knowledge, it's yours; no one can take that from you.

With that said, here are a few ways to make the most of each and every career opportunity, big or small. (What a great way to invest in yourself!):

- **Take a performance improvement perspective**

  Bringing an entrepreneurial spirit to any role can make you a better employee and help you enjoy your work more. If you are confident that a few changes would add to your or your team's productivity, pitch them to your boss and team members. Be sure to approach this from a positive perspective: changes that do not cost the company money and that can potentially improve financial performance are usually welcomed and appreciated.

- **Manage yourself**

  You are the master of your own career, so it is up to you to take steps to advance it and get the qualifications and experience that you need to move forward. Your employer does not owe this to you.

- **Seek out greatness**

  Look for projects where you can work with smart, successful, positive people. Too many people wait for opportunities to come knocking on their door (and then they're too busy texting to notice). Get out there and ask for your chance to learn from the people you admire; their greatness is often contagious, so soak it up, sunshine!

Make these practices your M.O., to help you get on track to serious career advancement. Way too many people become stagnant in a position, feeling they have little control over their own progress. Let them. Successful people put their best foot forward on each and every task, take a positive attitude, and are always on the lookout for opportunities to develop their abilities further.

To prove our point, take a good look around your workplace and see how many of your co-workers are actually taking this success-oriented approach. Once you identify those who do the minimum (a.k.a., the lazy, the unmotivated, and the grumblers), you might just find yourself standing alone, or at least in a pretty small group. That's opportunity. So step up and take action. You might just be surprised by the results.

**HINDSIGHT**

*I've always been a self-motivated person, and had big, long-term goals even at the beginning of my career. From time to time, I would come across co-workers and peers who would react very negatively to my personal career goals: "You're too young." "You don't have enough experience." "You shouldn't be focusing on long-term goals." "You won't get there." And so on.*

*Looking back, I realized that they were telling me more about their own experiences than what my own career could be. What a dreary existence to be so negative; no wonder they were so limited in their career progression! I don't know too many successful people who have a negative view of the world (can't think of any, actually); that's enough of a reason to take a positive attitude, believe in your own abilities, and get busy! It worked for me.*

## Being Let Go

There are many reasons why you might be cut loose from a job, and rest assured, the reasons may be more related to the company's financial position or corporate reorganization than your performance. However, if you were not performing up to par and really are to blame, it is critical to take honest stock of your role in the situation so that it will not be repeated. Really, you can't afford not to.

Regardless of the reason, it hurts. Even if you were expecting to lose your job, due to a department closure, for example, you are still going to experience some feelings of loss. This is a period of adjustment where you need support from others. Many employers offer career counselling as part of employees' severance packages. Even if it is difficult to do so, do not pass up this offer. Qualified counsellors can help you deal with the hurt, confusion, and anger that you may be experiencing, as well as help you move forward with your job search. So, be first in line and do what you can to approach this valuable resource with a positive attitude.

Don't be surprised if former employees do not contact you; they often don't know what to say and may feel survivor's guilt. Seek out the work friendships you want to maintain; apart from that, be civil, sincere, and professional; former colleagues can be your future references.

Here are some items to consider if you happen to find yourself on the wrong side of the employment equation:

- **Understand options for pension plans and retirement accounts**

  You may have the choice to leave your pension with the company or take a commuted value in a locked-in retirement account. The company should be able to provide a calculation for you, in terms of the value of either option.

- **Determine the status of professional and membership dues**

  During the course of your employment, the company may have paid professional and/or membership dues on your behalf. Inquire about the requirements to transfer these items to yourself personally, the remaining coverage periods, and whether or not you will be subject to reimbursing your employer for any of the amounts that have already been paid.

- **Determine your benefits-plan status**

  Find out what benefits, such as medical or dental, are preserved for the interim period before you find a new job. Ask your employer how long your benefits coverage will continue.

A good approach is to collect the information and not make any immediate decisions. Being let go can be a traumatic experience, and chances are you will not be thinking clearly in the early days of being unemployed. Gather the information and take the time to consider it fully; do your due diligence, and ask for advice. You will be glad you did.

## Severance Pay to Take Away the Sting

Severance pay, at a minimum, is generally government regulated in your jurisdiction, may be specified in your employment contract, or may be part of the company's policies. Severance pay can be based on years of service and may be subject to negotiation between the company and the departing employee. Given the circumstance, it is a good idea to get professional advice to better understand your position and options.

In terms of treatment of the cash, you may have the option to shelter this money in a retirement account, or to split the amount between this year and the next, in order to minimize the tax impact. You may also have the choice between receiving a lump-sum amount or an ongoing salary. If this is the case, consider your tax bracket and whether or not you will receive payments over more than one tax year.

The number-one mistake that people make with severance pay is to treat it like income. They deposit it into their chequing account and wonder what happened when it's all gone! If you receive severance pay, then you *need* a severance plan. This involves the following:

- eliminating all non-essential expenses;
- parking your severance pay away from your debit card, where it will be all too easily accessed on a daily, on-the-fly basis. That said, do put it in a savings account where you can access some or all of the funds, if necessary;
- lining up a flexible debt option, such as a low-interest line of credit;
- going on a "cash diet" for any emotional or controllable expenses, such as groceries, hair appointments, uncontrollable splurges at designer discount stores, and so on;
- mapping out how long your money will last in the event that you don't find immediate work, based on your reduced level of expenses; and

- making sure you understand the tax implications of severance pay, especially in terms of the net cash amount that you will receive. For example, it would be disappointing to make a plan based on $20,000 of net severance pay, only to find out that you are really working with a net cash amount of $10,000.

## Getting Back on that Horse

Once you've downed the Cab-Merlot with your pals and gone home to trash-talk your former employers until your dog is tired of hearing about it, it's time to think positively about your options.

Here's the good news: you are free! Let your imagination run wild with what you could accomplish and what your next career steps could be. Try to remember all those dreams about what you would rather have been doing while stuck in airless meeting rooms and confining cubicles. Take stock of your skills and brainstorm about the possibilities of applying those skills . . . elsewhere.

Even forced change can be a gift in disguise. For many people, being released from a job gives them a whole new outlook that ends up changing their life for the better. You may decide to take courses, start your own business, or move your career in a totally different direction. Take the opportunity to focus on becoming your best self, and what you need to do to get there.

Be open and tell people that you are facing a career change and what your interests are. You never know who is connected to whom, or what an idle conversation at the coffee bar could lead to (in fact, many jobs are never posted; they are just networked informally until a candidate is found). Networking groups, such as LinkedIn and other social groups, can help you connect to new contacts and get support from others. You might even be surprised to make valuable contacts in the most unlikely of places, such as the gym, the hair salon, or the grocery store lineup. Many a deal has been made whilst chatting about bulk food finds or sitting under a heat lamp (with foil-wrapped hair, every woman is an equal).

Think about yourself as a product for which you need to design a marketing plan—a compelling and desirable brand, baby.

A good approach is to understand all of your key skills and accomplishments; in this way, your competencies can be targeted to potential employment situations. For example, you might have spent your entire career thus far in the transportation industry, but once you clearly define your key competencies, you will notice that these skills can be applied to many industries. (Could that management career in the travel industry really be possible?) As part of this process, determine what, if any, training or professional development is needed to make a move. Do your research and sign up. It's a great way to make productive use of your time, get the training you need, and make contacts in the industry that interests you.

Updating your resumé is an important part of your personal marketing plan, so do it right. A modern approach is the skills-based resumé (rather than the more dated chronological job listing approach, though that still has its proponents).

There are an abundance of resources available to guide you through this process, and given that your resumé is often your first point of contact with a potential employer, it is worth the effort to prepare a strong one. Create a first draft and get some feedback from a human-resources professional or from friends who routinely hire staff. You might be surprised how much feedback they will have, because, yes, there are lots of poor resumés out there. Don't let yours be one of them!

From a financial perspective, manage your spending carefully and continue to follow a debt-repayment plan. Keep any lines of credit open and available in case an opportunity arises. (Say, Carla Bruni just called. She's looking for a cultural attaché and would like to interview you tomorrow afternoon in front of the Louvre in Paris?

Can you hop a flight? *Mais oui!*) Okay, now we're dreaming, but the principle's the same: by keeping yourself out of financial stress, you will be in the best position to take your time and make the right choice from the opportunities that come your way (a job in Paris hopefully being one of them).

Most importantly, remember that just because your job situation has changed, *you* have not changed. You are a compelling person with the same strengths, talents, smarts, and endearing sense of humour that you've always had. Who wouldn't love and find value in that?

---

 **LIFE LESSON: PROTECT YOUR RISK PROFILE,**
**BEFORE YOU RISK WALKING AWAY**

Ideally, before you make a career change, make sure your debt is as efficient as possible. Every time you experience a change in employer, it will take a while before you are deemed to be a good lending risk again. If your long-term plan is to start a business or be self-employed, it could take years to reclaim your risk "worthiness." Ensuring that you are financially agile before making a break can give you far more options and more freedom to pursue greater career and life opportunities!

# 5

## So Crazy, It Just Might Work

*Finance and Business*

### Taking the Plunge and Starting Your Own Business

Our dear friend Anna had a great corporate career going. Over twelve years, she had worked for two blue-chip companies and had risen to the level of managing director. She was respected by her peers, received great bonuses every year, and wore excellent suits (one of the true benefits of being part of the corporate world). This girl had really hit the big time—the stuff that dreams are made of—and her friends (like us) marvelled at Anna's success in the white-collar, often male-dominated world, even if we didn't see her much.

When we did see Anna, however, she seemed indifferent to her success. She liked her work, liked her colleagues, and felt proud of the company she worked for, but she often remarked that she "had no life." Reporting to her desk for 40 (okay, 60) some hours a week, taking projects home on weekends, plus being available at all hours on her mobile, left her with very little energy or time. There was no point in changing companies, she told us, as a new role would just require even more effort, and in the end, all the companies in her industry were pretty much the same.

What options did she have? Anna wasn't married and didn't have kids. Her savings were achieved primarily through payroll deductions and matching company savings plans. She had recently bought a home and absolutely relied on her biweekly paycheque to make her mortgage payments. She felt stuck: addicted to her corporate salary, hating those designer suits (oh, to wear yoga pants all day!), and becoming increasingly depressed.

One day, when the open-space floor plan at work got to be a little more rowdy than Anna could bear, she picked up her laptop and files and went home to finish a project. She set up at her kitchen table, and with her favourite music playing in the background, ploughed through her work. After a few hours of focused effort, her project was complete. Anna was pleased with her productivity, and since it was still light outside, she took a glass of wine and her thoughts out to her neglected garden, where she pulled a few weeds, mulled over some unresolved problems, and composed e-mails in her head.

As she returned to her laptop on the kitchen table, Anna looked around her beloved home (alas, it was greatly in need of dusting) and thought: *This is good! I could really get used to working from home.* Perhaps surprisingly, this was something that she had never given much thought to, as she spent so much effort just trying to keep up with all of the demands of corporate life. Goodness, she rarely even spent a solid hour *awake* at home, considering her exhaustive work, gym, social, and networking schedules. She started thinking.

Anna had worked on projects with self-employed consultants and always admired the way they seemed so, well, free. *Breezy,* even, and *happy.* They came and went, chose the projects they wanted to work on, never got caught in office politics, and charged an arm and a leg for their work. But Anna had never contemplated self-employment as an option for herself. *That's what people with husbands did,* she had told herself. *Starting your own business is for women with the luxury and stability of a second income, upon which they can rely. Too risky for me. I have a mortgage!*

Yet, on this day, Anna ignored the little naysayer voice in her head and began calculating what her company would have paid a consultant to do the project that she had just completed. She punched numbers into her calculator and scribbled the figures onto a hydro bill envelope that was lying next to her computer (embarrassingly, it had been there for months). Anna stared at the figures in awe. It was the equivalent to a month's salary. Then, she calculated how many hours she would have to work as a consultant to replace her annual salary. Much to Anna's interest, it was a lot fewer than she was currently working.

Anna made a list of all the people she knew in the industry who had contacted her in the past, asking for consultant referrals. She surprised herself with how broad her network was, just listing names off the top of her head. Anna dug a little deeper, and with some effort, she had developed quite an impressive list.

A new little voice in Anna's head began to softly whisper: *Maybe, I can do this. Maybe it isn't so crazy. Or maybe, it's so crazy, it just might work.*

## Timing and the Art of the Possible

Starting your own business (like love, lightning, and winning the lottery) is always about timing. Anna did not plan on becoming an entrepreneur until the right idea came to her, at the right time. At that point, everything that previously had seemed impossible suddenly seemed possible.

Sometimes, as in Anna's case, this can happen from an idea; in other instances, it can happen from reaching a point where the status quo just doesn't cut it anymore. You realize that you can't get through another all-night working session; feel held back by your work; or simply cannot stand another project assignment with the world's most annoying co-worker (does this guy *ever* stop talking? Must she take credit for *everything?*).

Or perhaps you're a lot like Anna (driven and smart), but your circumstances aren't. Many a mom has found her creativity kicks in just as the baby kicks its way out. Many a divorcing woman has found that she's ready to fuel her future, on her own terms, just as she kicks him out the door. Many a downsized woman (as in "laid off," not post-diet) has found that exploring being in business for herself beats the interview junket for jobs that just don't seem very compelling. And many a retired woman has found that, love him as she might, that annoying co-worker has now been replaced by an annoying husband (a girl just needs an outlet once in a while!). And, thus, self-employment is born.

But change takes time. There are many things in your life that will seem to hold you back from taking action, whether it's starting a business, saving for a vacation, or losing a few extra pounds. You can always find reasons why "now is not the time." Fortunately, your innermost desires will not take no for an answer forever. When you really need and want to achieve something in your life, you will find your circumstances shifting to position yourself for the opportunity, despite any excuses you tell yourself, in terms of why you *can't* possibly do it.

Like many first-time entrepreneurs, the idea that would eventually develop into Anna's successful consulting business, started out with a few figures scratched on the back of an envelope (or on the cover of a phone book, or in the margins of a takeout pizza menu, or on a cocktail napkin . . . just to name a few real-life examples).

The point when an idea starts to take form and your mind starts to shift to the realization that this might be possible is an exciting and important phase of your business development. Allow yourself to think big, to brainstorm many scenarios, to imagine what you would do if you knew you would not fail (don't worry—there will be *lots* of opportunities for reality checks later on in the process).

Being an entrepreneur requires you to be open to possibilities, to look for a niche market opportunity and fill it, or to create something where there was nothing before. Most importantly, it provides you with the chance to use your knowledge and your strengths to build something for *yourself.*

So while dreaming about the possibilities, enjoy the rush and don't hasten the process. You will need the momentum of strong, positive energy and unshakeable faith in your capabilities to push you through the hard work that follows. Many people think about business opportunities for months or even years before launching a business, and it sometimes takes a while for the pieces to fall into place, whether they are particular developments in the marketplace or within your own skill set. So, take it all in and keep moving forward.

What is that saying about inspiration versus perspiration? Oh yeah, Thomas Alva Edison once said, "Genius is 1 per cent inspiration and 99 per cent perspiration." Well that may be true, but you don't perspire, now do you? You *glow.*

Well get ready, honey, because there is about to be a whole lot of *glowing* going on!

 **DID YOU KNOW? IT'S PORTABLE, BABY**

Although corporate life might give you lots of headaches and sleepless nights, it also provides an excellent foundation for building something for yourself. Think about it: large corporations spend significant amounts of money developing systems and processes (great examples of how to do things), training programs (to teach you new skills), and marketing strategies (to demonstrate what works well to attract clients). Not to mention, all of the experience you gained working on a wide range of assignments, as well as that address book full of contacts.

*(continued)*

> The beauty of this is that it's all portable: the skills, experience, and insight that you gained can travel with you in your knowledge base for your next venture. Of course, be mindful of any limitations in your employment agreement and other corporate and/or work policies, but for the most part, the great experience you gained is your own. So, use it!

## Business Start-up Structures

When starting a business, there are plenty of considerations to take into account. The first decision to make, once you determine the particular nature of the business, is the structure in which to carry on your business. There are various vehicles: a sole proprietorship, a partnership, or a corporation:

- **Sole proprietorship**

  This is simply one person carrying on business. This approach is often attractive in its simplicity, but the owner/operator has unlimited liability.

  Examples of a sole proprietorship could include a cleaner, repair person, consultant, or freelance editor.

- **Partnership**

  A partnership is simply the relationship existing between two or more persons carrying on business together with a view to profit and is a relatively simple and inexpensive organization to create and maintain, as compared to a corporation. There are, however, drawbacks to a partnership, including the fact that each partner is personally liable to almost the full extent of his or her personal and business assets and for all debts and obligations of the partnership.

Although there are certain tax advantages available to shareholders of a corporation that are not available to members of a partnership, one advantage of a partnership is that partnership losses can be applied to the taxpayer's personal income tax return. As well, in the absence of a partnership agreement dictating otherwise, a partnership is terminated upon the death of a partner, which can be an effective resolution approach.

Examples of a partnership could include construction, professional services, and investment companies.

- **Corporation**

A corporation is a separate legal entity controlled by its shareholders who elect directors who are responsible for supervising and administering the corporation's affairs. The directors appoint officers (i.e., president, secretary, and so on) who are responsible for the day-to-day running of the corporation.

There are various advantages and disadvantages to incorporation. The advantages include:

- **Limited liability:** A shareholder of a corporation is usually only liable to the extent of his or her actual investment or the amount of any loan made to the corporation.

- **Tax advantages:** Taxes may be minimized or deferred, and additional types of deductions may be permitted.

- **Exists in perpetuity:** A corporation is unaffected by the lives of the individual shareholders, and exists until it is wound-up or dissolved.

- **Capital acquisition:** In general terms, banks and financial institutions like working with corporations; however, be aware that they may want personal guarantees when providing financing to a company.

The disadvantages include:

- **Costs:** A corporation is costly to start and entails additional ongoing costs, such as filing and financial statement audit expenditures.

- **No transfer of tax losses to individuals:** Individual shareholders cannot use the corporation's losses as part of their personal tax returns, as a corporation is a separate legal entity.

- **Administration requirements:** There are formal yearly administrative requirements, including annual returns and separate income tax returns for the business. Meetings of directors and shareholders must be held annually.

Examples of a corporation could include large, established businesses, situations where there are multiple shareholders who have come together to establish a business, and circumstances where the advantages of incorporating fit well with the needs and objectives of the founder(s).

Some jurisdictions may require incorporation for certain types of businesses or professions, so it's important to get the right advice to understand any requirements or limitations in this regard.

When starting a business, it is important to consider the most appropriate structure. Qualified advisors, such as business advisors (who typically bring expertise in managing a company), lawyers, and accountants, can provide assistance to help you make a sound decision based on your personal situation and business needs.

## From Back of the Envelope to Business Plan

Once you've had sufficient time to brainstorm and consider the great possibilities for your business, it's time to hunker down and figure out what is actually feasible and achievable—and in what order. Many a brilliant entrepreneurial idea has crashed because the business strategy was not thought out or was poorly executed. Furthermore, many fail to estimate the amount of work, time, expense, and commitment that launching, executing, and building a *profitable* business will take (think *years*, not months).

Consider the following:

- **Your time, effort, and resources**

    Your business is likely going to require a lot of time, effort, and money on your part in order to get off the ground, so before you start charging down the runway, it's important that you get a sense of whether or not the business has a realistic chance of being successful, as well as the amount of financial assistance that you may require from others in order to make it happen.

- **Your ability to get financial support from others**

    Many businesses require financial support beyond that of the founders to get started, and growing businesses tend to require additional capital to support the increased costs of serving more customers and expanding their brand reach. Whether potential sources of capital are friends and family or financial institutions, you will have to be able to demonstrate the financial potential of your business, as well as the strategy that you will employ to get there.

    Financial partners (i.e., lending institutions, angel investors, or venture capital firms) have specific needs in this regard, so it's key to understand what they are in order to have a realistic chance at securing their support.

## Rock-Solid Business Planning

The first step toward turning your idea into reality is to create a rock-solid business plan. This is a comprehensive document that fully explains the concept of your business, the strategy you will use to execute it, and the estimated financial results from doing so (as well as the amount of capital required and the use of funds). In order to put together a good business plan, you will have to answer many important questions. As a means of introduction, think of it in terms of the five Ws and the big H:

1. **Who**—you and anyone else who may be involved in the business:
   - ✓ What are the key roles and responsibilities?
   - ✓ What skills and experience do the founders bring to the company?
   - ✓ Why are these skills important?
   - ✓ Are there gaps in the management team and how will they be addressed?

2. **What**—a concise but thorough description of your business concept:
   - ✓ What is the product or service?
   - ✓ What are the key features and benefits?
   - ✓ How is your product or service better than what is currently available in the marketplace?

3. **When**—how long it will take you to start operating the company:
   - ✓ What will operations look like in one year?
   - ✓ In three years?
   - ✓ In five years?

4. **Where**—the location of your operations and the particulars of your facility, which are important for manufacturing- and processing-related businesses:

✓ What is the production capacity of your facility?

✓ Are other locations required?

✓ What do you expect your capital expenditures to be in order to keep the facility running well?

5. **Why**—market research that details the opportunity, describes your competitors, and demonstrates your business's viability is critical. Key areas to consider include:

✓ A description of the markets that your business would serve, such as their location, and characteristics.

✓ Is the market large enough to generate the level of sales that your business requires in order to be successful?

✓ Why would customers choose to do business with you, as opposed to your competitors?

6. **How**—your strategy for building the business and how you plan to get your product to market. Customers will not simply line up to buy, just because your business has launched. It takes a significant amount of effort to make potential customers aware of your business, as well as to get your product in the hands of customers. As such, you must consider and detail in writing:

✓ your marketing strategy;

✓ distribution; and

✓ the cost of each new customer or lead acquisition over time.

Your business plan should also outline the financial aspects of your company, including the estimated financial results from operating the business over a three-to-five-year period. If you plan to borrow funds to get started, you need to clarify the estimated amount of financing that you are looking for, how this amount has been determined, and a description of how you will use those funds.

A business plan is imperative to help you analyze whether a good idea can become a serious and viable enterprise, which is particularly important if you require the business to generate sufficient cash flow to support your personal financial needs. It will also serve as a guide; that is, a document you can refer back to again and again in your early days of setting up operations. This is critical, as the day-to-day aspects of business can have many twists and turns that will distract you from the overall plan.

However, it is not simply a document for your eyes only. If you need investors or financial partners in order to get the business up and running (whether it's a bank or your dear old dad), you're going to need a professional business plan to make your case.

And while it may seem *totally* tedious and pointless (who reads all this anyway?), banks, investors, and financial partners *do* read business plans in full. They have seen innumerable plans—most not so good—and have specific needs in terms of information requirements and format.

And if (like many of us) you haven't a clue of the typical format, consider yourself to be more of a talker, or just need a good ol' kick in the pants, seek out help to write a professional business plan (on-line templates and/or business consultants can help).

## The Takeaway

Financial partners will always want to see your plan in writing. Those handwritten notes on your daughter's note pad? Nope, that won't impress them much. You have to put in the work to see the rewards.

---

 **GOLDEN RULE: DO YOUR MARKET RESEARCH**

Build your case for investors and increase your own confidence in the business concept by thoroughly researching and determining

*(continued)*

who your customers will be, why they will buy your product or service, and how much they will pay for it. Market research is essential in making the case as to why your business will succeed.

For example, find out who is already selling similar products in your own market, their prices or rates, their profitability, and their market share. Just because your business may not appear to have any identical competitors does not mean that there is no competition. There can be many ways to satisfy a particular market need, so investigate your competition thoroughly.

If you can point to a successful business that mirrors your own in another market (and is, therefore, not a competitor), include this example in your business plan as well. It's a model for your potential success!

---

 **HINDSIGHT**

*In the first year of running my own business, I worked harder and longer hours than I ever did as an employee at my previous corporate job. While I theoretically had more "freedom" and "flexibility," this mostly translated into the freedom to work in my gym clothes (though no time to actually go to the gym!) and the flexibility of responding to e-mails from my bed before falling asleep.*

*I spent every waking hour making sure my new clients were happy and well served, while actively marketing my services to potential clients. I also had to make sure that all of the administrative needs of my business were covered, including buying office supplies, filing information and tax requirements, and getting my financial statements done on time. When the contracts started flowing in, I was afraid to say no to any work for fear that I might not have*
(continued)

*any opportunities the next month. When you are self-employed, you are constantly driven by a compulsion to "make hay while the sun shines."*

*And as for rest and taking it easy after "work hours"? Ha, that's for the salaried people, I started to think. But hey, at least I get my grocery shopping done when there's no lineup in sight, and a "bad hair day" can mean a "stay in bed and work day." You gotta love that!*

## Please, Send Me an Angel

Ah, the quest for financing. Don't think that just because you're chasing money on behalf of your business, that it will be any easier to snag than it is for your personal bank account. In order to convince an investor to provide your start-up company with capital, you have to sell your plan (and your capability of pulling it off) as an attractive, *money-generating* investment. Investors part with their money when they feel confident that they will get it back, along with a healthy return. (Otherwise, it wouldn't be called "investing"; it would be called "a hand out.")

Raising capital for an early-stage business is a lot more difficult than most people imagine. Odds are that it will take much longer than you anticipate, and you will likely raise less money than you hoped to secure (and give away more equity). Do not let this dissuade you. What this means is that you must be *extra-professional* and *extra-prepared* with a very well-honed business plan in order to increase your chance at wooing an investor.

Many business owners seek the assistance of qualified advisors to help them refine their business plans, as well as to help make introductions to potential investors. Business advisors, accountants, investment advisors, and lawyers with direct experience in corporate law and raising capital can all be helpful in finding you potential investors. The reality of the situation is, however, that too many would-be entrepreneurs fail to get the right assistance from advisors who could really help their cause. Instead, they stubbornly (or naively) cling to their idea and resist good advice to help make it viable. Smart entrepreneurs, on the other hand, seek out the best assistance they can find.

Remember, there is no weakness in asking for help. Everyone has strengths and weaknesses, so it's not about knowing all of the answers, but rather, taking the necessary steps to get the right information from those who have the knowledge and experience.

## A Snapshot of Early-Stage Investors

Start-up or early-stage businesses have their own unique challenges that make it difficult for conventional financial partners, such as banks and other traditional lenders, to participate in a significant way. Young businesses lack cash flow (to repay loans), often focus on emerging products and markets, and may have inexperienced management teams. As a result, it is necessary to identify potential financial partners who are better matched to this type of situation.

Investors and financial partners in the early stage typically include:

- **founders, friends, and family** who invest their money to support the efforts and dreams of those who are close to them;
- **angel investors,** high-net-worth individuals who support young businesses, often out of their own personal interest in seeing a particular product, service, or technology move forward;
- **government programs** that support business start-ups or growth with grants, loans, tax credits, and other types of assistance;

- **venture capitalists,** investors who concentrate on young companies with high growth potential; and
- **banks and credit unions** that provide business accounts and overdraft protection. In the case of early-stage businesses, this type of financial institution typically does not play a significant role.

Investments in the early stage may come in the form of:

- **grants** where funding is provided and is *not* repayable, as long as certain terms and conditions are met;
- **loans** where the company is provided with funding that is repayable over a specific period of time, based on particular terms (i.e., payment, interest rate, etc.). Loans are typically provided for a specific purpose, such as the purchase of an asset, and may require collateral in order to be obtained;
- **equity** that provides investors with shares in the company in exchange for capital. Shares may be in the form of common shares, which allow investors to share in the financial performance of the company, as well as in the risk of ownership; or preferred shares, which do not participate in the performance of the company, but rather are compensated with a fixed return, such as a dividend, and have preference in terms of repayment, as compared to common shares; and
- **some combination of the above.**

In general terms, financing and investment structuring are fairly complex topics. As we've drilled into you repeatedly in this chapter, but bears repeating, it is a good idea to seek out qualified professional advice to help you understand the various options and their implications as they relate to your business structure, your personal financial situation, and the overall equity picture you envision.

## Angel Investors versus Venture Capitalists

Angel investors . . . ah, someone must have sent you from above!

*Angel investors* are aptly named for their tendency to rescue a start-up business owner who can't seem to get anywhere with the bank or other potential sources of financing.

Indeed, an angel investor is typically an affluent individual who is willing to take a chance on helping you get your business started, often as a result of their own personal interest in or knowledge of a particular product, service, or technology. The investor may give you capital in return for a stake in the business, or he or she may provide you with a loan, with expectations of interest and a repayment schedule.

*Venture capitalists*, on the other hand, manage money for a pool of investors, which could include individuals or institutions. They typically have a defined investment strategy, in terms of particular industries in which the venture capitalist would invest, the stage of development, geographic region, and the size of investment.

A venture capitalist often works closely with the management teams of the companies in which the fund invests, as a means of protecting their investment and increasing the likelihood of generating a good return.

Search your community for angel networks, angel-investment groups, or venture capital firms that are looking for the right opportunity to part with their money. There is often no easy way to find potential investors, as raising capital has a significant relationship component, so you have to get out there and start meeting people. As with much in life, a little networking goes a long way. You never know who a new friend, colleague, or acquaintance knows or could introduce you to.

Do recognize that both angel and venture capital funding are typically not easy to attract, given the sheer volume of potential investment opportunities, as well as the specific selection criteria of investors. But as any entrepreneur will tell you, being undercapitalized is one of the easiest ways to guarantee business failure . . . so work that room!

 **HINDSIGHT**

*For whatever reason, working with entrepreneurs can be like herding cats; they scramble this way and that, chasing after any new idea that rolls by. Focus can be a real challenge.*

*The smart entrepreneurs, however, are the ones who can focus; who recognize that they don't know it all and are willing to take advice. These are the ones who are often the most successful, as they are willing to take feedback to heart and use it to improve what they can do; they recognize that this only makes them better.*

*What's more, this is an attribute that investors and financial partners really value, as most have no interest in working with entrepreneurs who are not coachable. Business is hard enough as it is; who wants to fight a battle every time a good suggestion is put forward.*

## Are You Buying Yourself a Job?

Let's start at square one when asking this very important question: do you require this business to support your personal income requirements? Or will the income that will (hopefully) be generated from the business be more of a part-time, second income, or hobby venture at least to start?

This is extremely important to understand well, as potential business owners often get so caught up in bringing their great idea to fruition, that they don't pay attention to the financial realities of the situation.

As a result, they rack up huge overhead costs, telling themselves that "it takes money to make money" (always a dangerous motto) and assuring everyone around them that the money will soon come rolling in once the business takes off (heard that one before).

Despite what many people think, profits are not the only motivator to starting a business. Maybe you want to turn your farmhouse into a bed and breakfast to help cover the mortgage and maintenance costs. Or, perhaps you want to plant some old French grapevines in your garden because it's always been a dream to make your own wine. Some businesses are more pleasure-oriented than others and many people are satisfied with breaking even (or not!) on their business venture. They're in it for the experience, for the pride of ownership, and maybe even to add a notch to their career—and life—belts.

Understanding your own intentions for your business is paramount. In this way, you can grow your business (or limit its growth) to levels that suit your lifestyle and your goals for how you want to live your life and expand your career. For some people, turning a pleasurable pastime into an overwhelming job takes all the fun out of it. For others, the ability to share their passion with others (even if it means more work) only increases their joy and satisfaction.

So . . . do you have a need to build a business that will replace your employment salary or is your venture more about choice and less about income? Here are a few important questions to help you get to the heart of the matter:

- ✓ Do you need the business to generate a certain amount of cash to support your income requirements?
- ✓ Does the business require a full-time focus?
- ✓ Are you counting on the business to generate sufficient cash flow to replace your employment salary?

✓ Is there a market need for your product or service that is large enough to build a business around?

✓ Will your business respond to specific products and services that customers want and need?

✓ Are you aware of your competitors and does your business have the ability to successfully compete and differentiate itself?

✓ Are you on top of industry and market trends and developments?

✓ Would you hire the best people you could find to work with you?

If you answered yes to the majority of the questions above, you likely have a strong need for the business to generate a sufficient amount of money to support your personal income requirements. In order to be successful, it is important that the business's product or service is in line with what customers want and is competitive, in terms of quality and price. As a result, businesses of this nature are more focused on the opportunities in the marketplace and needs of customers, as opposed to doing what is most convenient for the business leader.

If, on the other hand, you answered no to most of the questions above, chances are, you don't require or intend that the business have a specific income-generating ability to replace your employment income. As a result, these types of businesses tend to be more lifestyle-oriented and built around the needs of the business leader, as opposed to the needs of the marketplace. The risk with this type of company is that a more market-focused competitor can easily swoop in and steal your customers with lures of better prices, emerging and current products, and more efficient service. For business leaders who depend on their company to satisfy their personal income requirements, this can represent a significant and unacceptable degree of risk.

Furthermore, while not always the case, a more market-driven business has generally given thought to a future exit strategy, in terms of how the company may be acquired in full or in part at a later date, and has built its structure and operations around this possibility. A more lifestyle-driven business, on the other hand, typically focuses on the individual and her skill set as the (often irreplaceable) service provider, thus making an acquisition opportunity less likely.

---

 **LIFE LESSON: PROFIT FIRST, THEN VOLUME**

Forgive us if we are being obvious, but you would be surprised how many business owners race to expand a money-losing venture. We are here to warn you that if you are losing money on each transaction, you certainly won't make up for it by increasing your volume. Here's what you need to keep in mind in the early stages: start small, refine your product, adjust your service, and get acquainted with your business processes and pricing model. *Dominate* your market category (and targeted geographic region).

Once you have figured out the range in which you can earn a profit on every single unit of your sales, only then should you expand to bigger volumes.

---

## First the Business Plan, Then the Operational Guide

Your business plan was the guiding force to help get your business off the ground. Once you're in motion, however, it is necessary to have an operational strategy as to *how* you will achieve the objectives of your business plan on a day-to-day basis. Think about it: these two aspects are really quite different, as the business plan is more strategic in nature, while the day-to-day plan requires much more of an in-the-field approach.

As such, the elements of your operational plan should include:

- **organizational chart of key positions** to identify the various roles, as well as who works together and what the reporting relationships are;

- **job descriptions for all positions** including a summary of the key responsibilities and qualifications for holding each position;

- **marketing and distribution plan** of how products will get to customers, as well as the company's advertising and promotion plans and pricing structure;

- **production plan** to ensure that products are generated according to a standard and on a timely basis. This is critical to plan for, particularly as sales volumes increase;

- **financial plan,** including budgets, accounting systems, and internal financial statements and reports. It is critical that the financial system be structured to yield accurate and timely financial information and be staffed by people who have the necessary skills and expertise (this is not the role to assign to a friend or relative who has more enthusiasm than experience).

Business owners learn the lessons of their trade through years of practice and often through trial and error. A strong business leader delivers much more than merely a product or service; she must excel at managing people, guiding the processes, and staying on top of the financial and administrative aspects of the company. That's a big job!

 **GOLDEN RULE: IF IT CAN GO WRONG, IT PROBABLY WILL**

Although entrepreneurs might just be the most optimistic people on the face of the earth, let's face it: running a company is one tough

(*continued*)

business. It is a tall order, even for those with significant business experience and qualifications, and experienced business leaders recognize this fact.

Too many entrepreneurs, however, seem to brush it off: it doesn't apply to me; everyone will want my product; once the business gets started, it will work itself out; and so on. But trust us: if it can go wrong, it probably will. In fact, once you are in business, you will have things go wrong that you never even dreamed to be a possibility ("But I thought she would be my star employee!"), so it pays to be prepared.

Seek out qualified advice, listen, and think about how to make your business concept as risk-proof as possible. Keep your enemies close and your advisors closer!

 **DID YOU KNOW? "YOU COMPLETE ME" FOR BUSINESS**

Being an entrepreneur and being a business manager are very different skill sets. One takes pleasure in the big picture: coming up with new ideas, finding investors, selling an idea, and bringing a concept to life.

Running the day-to-day operations with payroll, production lines, and cash-flow issues, requires an entirely *different* type of focus. This is why many people prefer to work as a team, with business partners that have complementary strengths and skill sets. Together, they can give the business everything that it needs to be successful.

## The Partner Pre-nup

If you choose to go into business with a partner, it is smart to establish a shareholders' agreement before you get started. Think of this as a rulebook for how the business will be run, as well as a guide for resolving the inevitable conflicts and questions that will arise during the course of the business's lifetime.

For example, what happens if your partner gets divorced and her angry ex-husband still owns part of your business? This type of situation has hamstrung many a company until the paper throwing subsides and life can get back to normal. But will the business have survived the ordeal?

A strong shareholders' agreement will help to address these types of situations, as well as ensure that you don't end up in business with someone you did not (or would never) choose as a partner, forcing you to close the doors because of an unfortunate personal situation. Much like a pre-nup, a shareholders' agreement protects the interests of both (or all) parties, provides financial security for the owners, and can preserve the continuity of a business in the face of ownership change. These agreements are best developed at the outset, when everyone is excited about going forward and generally in a good mood. In this way, should that mood dissipate as you move forward (as it so often does), the agreement will be in place and the various bumps along the way can be smoothed out by simply referring to what was agreed to at the start.

A well-designed shareholders' agreement will address the outcomes for many common situations that may occur over the course of operating a business, such as the:

- death of a shareholder;
- disability of a shareholder;
- sale or transfer of shares to a third party;
- retirement of a shareholder;
- divorce of a shareholder;
- loss of professional credentials, and legal or financial problems;

- termination of employment of a shareholder;
- bankruptcy of a shareholder; and
- disagreements between shareholders.

Although some of these areas might be difficult to imagine at the outset, a qualified legal advisor can help to develop a shareholders' agreement that will identify the key areas to outline in writing, with the aim of keeping your business operating smoothly should the unexpected occur.

You might also want to consider an insurance policy to help fund any buy-sell provisions should one partner become incapacitated or die. Discuss your options with a licensed insurance professional.

## The Takeaway

You should discuss what to do if things go wrong or not as expected before a crisis actually occurs. Despite the axiom, business *does* get personal rather quickly, so it's best to lay the ground rules before any clouded judgment or traumatic event gets in the way. By making the effort to set the rules up front, you are enabling yourself and your partner(s) to focus on running and growing the *business* going forward. And that's where the focus should be all along, now isn't it?

 **GOLDEN RULE: THE BUCK STOPS WITH YOU**

Despite your best intentions, being in business can be a lot more difficult than expected. Sales often do not materialize as quickly as hoped, which can cause cash flow problems and result in taking steps backwards, such as reducing staffing levels or closing office space.

*(continued)*

On the other hand, your business might grow so rapidly that additional financing is required to support that growth. For example, you may need to purchase more inventory, acquire better technology, hire more staff, or have a need for extra working capital while receivables are being collected.

Either way, changes to your cash flow and the financing requirements of the business will fluctuate, which can be stressful. Being prepared for the ebbs and flows is an essential part of successful business management. As the business leader, you are ultimately responsible for smoothly handling the capital requirements of the business, so make it a priority to run your company well to keep investors and financial partners happy, as well as to seek out advisors who can help you to stay on top of the important task of raising additional capital (for many, it's an ongoing, and often draining, task).

 **DID YOU KNOW? GET IT OUT OF YOUR HEAD AND INTO REALITY**

If you intend to sell your company one day, you need to run it in a way that is attractive and valuable to a potential purchaser. If the business fully depends on you for its existence (all the trade secrets are locked in a vault inside your head), then the enterprise will be of much less value to a buyer who will have to start from scratch to figure it out. Why would they pay money for your business? Is there really anything to buy?

To make your company more saleable, make sure you build it in a transparent and well-documented way, ideally with well-trained staff who know exactly what they are doing. As such, the business is not dependent on the business leader and can be transferred to someone else. That's value for a purchaser and money in your pocket!

## Turning Points in Your Business

Managing a company for the long term means continuously evaluating your business's future prospects, as well as your own personal interest and commitment. Being a business leader can be challenging at the best of times and it is not uncommon for interests and energy to wane, notwithstanding the developments that may be occurring within the industry and local marketplace.

Here are some things to consider when evaluating your ongoing interest in leading the company, as well as the industry and market potential for the business:

- **The industry:**

    ✓ Where is the industry headed?

    ✓ Are there game-changing trends and developments underway or changes in technology that could radically alter the way in which business will be done?

    ✓ Will it be necessary to undertake a significant amount of research and development to keep up with the trends?

    ✓ Does the business need to raise capital in order to undertake the necessary enhancements?

    The answers to these questions will help you to get a sense of what the future holds, in terms of whether your products and services are still desirable to consumers or whether they are becoming obsolete or in need of a serious overhaul.

- **The competition:**

    ✓ Is the overall number of competitors in your marketplace growing or shrinking?

    ✓ Is it becoming more difficult to retain market share?

✓ Are large, new competitors coming into the local marketplace?

✓ Are prices being driven too low for profitability to be achieved?

✓ Are competitors consolidating (i.e., merging or being acquired) and what does this trend mean for your business?

Understanding the competitive landscape can help you to assess whether or not your business has a good opportunity to remain profitable and viable, or whether margins are being eroded and threatening future operations.

- **The "me" factor:**

✓ Do you still enjoy being in the business?

✓ Are you able to keep up with the pace?

✓ Do you have qualified employees to help you?

✓ Are you still passionate about this business?

Your continued interest in and commitment to running the business are important: either you have the interest to remain at the helm; or you need to consider other options, such as mentoring staff members to step up, bringing in a replacement, or perhaps selling the business.

## Is It Time to Sell, Walk Away, or Close Shop?

Based on the answers to the questions above, your business will either look viable for the foreseeable future, or perhaps, it is time to sell, walk away, or close the doors.

Changes in the industry, the market, and your own personal situation can lead you to consider critical turning points that must be addressed in order to protect your business, as well as the value you have built up in developing it. Failure to consider the impact of sweeping industry changes, for example, will leave you with a business that gets left behind and lacks relevance, resulting in the value you have built in the company being swept away with the tide.

When contemplating the future of your business, here are some options to consider:

- **Continue to grow the business as a standalone company**

  This option is really only viable for companies that have a good market opportunity, in terms of relevant products, sufficient margins, competent management, and good success in combating competitors (a gold star for those of you who qualify!).

- **Consider bringing in a partner to help**

  Bringing on a qualified partner to provide access to an expanded range of business, in terms of an enhanced product offering or larger customer base, can help to increase the revenue and longevity of a company. This approach can also bring additional management skills or perhaps provide a succession option down the road.

- **Consider merging with another business**

  A merger can provide the benefits of bringing on a partner, but often on a larger scale. A merger could mean additional locations, a complementary line of business, or a full management team as an option for succession. Building a larger business in this manner can also position the company for being an acquisition target at some point in the future.

- **Sell the business**

  If you lack the interest to take the business forward, either as it is or in an expanded manner, or if industry and market developments suggest that the business's future may be in question, selling the company may be your best option (you just have to hope there is a buyer). There are countless issues related to selling a business, and engaging qualified advisors (i.e., in law, tax, valuation, and business sale) is important to ensure that all of the important matters are addressed. In particular, if your business is truly in a "time to sell" situation, time really is of the essence to ensure that you can undertake a transaction quickly and get out as much of the value as possible.

· **Wind up the business**

Sometimes, companies reach a point where they are no longer financially viable or don't have value to anyone else, perhaps due to falling behind the needs of customers and no longer being relevant. In these situations, there is not an operating business that can be transferred to someone else, either because it does not operate well or is of no value to another party.

In these situations, the only option may be to wind up the business, which is largely a legal process. In the course of a wind up, the remaining assets of the company are sold on a best-efforts basis. Once the liabilities or obligations of the business have been met, the remaining proceeds, if any, are distributed to the shareholders and the business is wound up and no longer exists.

Recognize that should you opt to move forward with a growth plan, you may require additional financing or a modification of your business strategy to make it sustainable for the long term. Either way, this will likely mean updating the business plan to guide the company's strategy and growth efforts. Are you up for the challenge? Do you believe that you will be able to attract financial partners? These questions are important to consider when determining your next steps.

## The Takeaway

Being in business is all about cycles: things change, patterns emerge, and the focus on meeting market needs and beating the competition is always present. Would-be entrepreneurs might think that being in business for yourself represents the ultimate freedom, and although it does bring some flexibility, you can't get away from the fundamentals. If you're in business, it's all about evaluating, then *re-evaluating*, reshaping, retooling, and plain old getting it done!

And while many businesses fail, many also succeed. In terms of wealth generation, think of the *really* financially successful people you know. Business owners, right? You can see why more women are stepping up to the entrepreneurial plate. (They don't call it entrepren*her* for nothing!)

# 6

## The Big-Ticket Items of Life

*Finance and Major Purchases*

### Your House, Your Car, that Perfect Cottage in the Woods

If you're anything like us, long before you buy a house, a car, or
that perfect cottage in the woods, you've spent many an afternoon
daydreaming about what it's going to be like, how it's going to *feel*.
Ahhh . . . a sunny porch where you can sip your brew, a lovely garden
where the kids can play, or a sweet ride to zip around town in style.

Yes, major purchases are not just major in terms of cost; they're
also major because they are so *emotional*, representing the culmina-
tion of our dreams, desires, and attitudes about how we want to live
our lives—not only now, but in the future. They also encompass that
uniquely female perspective of rounding up friends and family to
share in that perfect home, vehicle, or holiday escape (or at least,
share their opinion!).

And yet, as with everything in life, what you dream of and what
is realistic *right now* might be two very different things. Compromise
is almost always required, and sometimes, that can be so difficult to
accept. But think about it this way: even if you can't quite achieve
your perfect dream home or the ultimate roadster (just yet), each

major purchase is a stepping stone, and a decision that will affect your future choices and opportunities. The end result? It pays to be in the know, consider your options, and balance both short- and long-term needs, from the starter home to the Tudor estate (and everything in between).

In this chapter, we will look at some of the big purchases of life: your home, your vehicle, your vacation escape, and investment properties.

## The Five Cs of an Attractive Borrower

"Neither a borrower, nor a lender be," wrote Shakespeare, who clearly must have had a few gold coins in his pocket when he bought his cottage in Stratford-upon-Avon. Most of us, however, are not equipped with the necessary amount of cash to buy a home or car outright (modern life can be so expensive!) and we instead rely on banks and lending institutions to help us with our major purchases. For many of us, borrowing is a part of life, which is all the more reason to be informed.

Let's start by considering how lenders will view *you* (yes, you!) when you are looking for important financing. Too often, we are so busy measuring the rooms and perusing paint chips that we forget that there are a few really important steps required to make that big purchase a reality, the most important being how to secure the best mortgage. It's kind of like a job interview: you have to be prepared and you have to present yourself well.

To keep it simple, here are the five Cs that lenders look for in potential borrowers:

### 1. Capacity

Once all of your other debts are added up, how much room do you have left to handle more debt, based on your income?

Can you actually handle more debt? Lending institutions typically have limits, in terms of the specific percentage of your income that can be allocated to total debts or housing costs, so in order to qualify, you have to fall within these guidelines. You might be able to influence the final outcome, however, by paying down existing debts or choosing a less expensive purchase in order to make the payment fit within the range.

## 2. Capital

With major purchases, it is not uncommon for buyers to put down some of their own cash at the time of the sale. How much cash can you put down on the purchase? Think of a down payment as your initial stake in the game: you're a safer bet in terms of financing if you pay more up front, and you'll pay less in interest later on.

## 3. Collateral

When you make a major purchase, it is often used to *secure* the loan. How valuable and marketable is your purchase? For example, is your dream home in good condition and in a desirable neighbourhood, or is it a real "fixer-upper" in a remote location? In case you default on the loan (which we know you would never do, of course), the lender wants to know how easy it would be to sell the asset to pay off the outstanding loan balance.

## 4. Character

This criterion really does relate directly to you. Are you a fine, upstanding citizen with a steady job, good education, and a stable place to live? (Now flash that irresistible smile!) Your reputation and earning capability mean a lot, so this is an example of where all your hard work to build up your character, your career, and your credit rating can really pay off.

### 5. Credit

When it comes to major purchases, you will often require experience with credit in order to get a larger amount. Do you have a history of making your credit payments on time and in full? A credit bureau report, credit score, or other lending references will provide proof of your track record, so you might as well fess up to any indiscretions now.

Although it might be frustrating and stressful, managing your credit is just a part of life. The more years that you can maintain a good record by ensuring that payments are made on time and by retiring debt, the better off you will be in terms of qualifying for future loans. Even if you're still young and not ready to make a major purchase, you should still be thinking ahead to the future when you *will* be ready (and believe us, that day will come!). After all, you wouldn't want that little problem of an unpaid department store card (gee, the balance was only $150) to get in the way of your dream home, now would you? We didn't think so! So, let's get to it . . .

## Your Home

Once upon a time, buying a house was a rite of passage for couples and newlyweds. Nowadays, home buying is no longer strictly for twosomes. Plenty of singletons are pooling their resources in order to buy a home that they could not afford individually, or buying a home that has divided units to provide a rental-income stream. Not only that, more and more women are buying homes and condos on their own (and then becoming permanent fixtures in the hardware-store aisles), making the choice to move forward with their dreams, instead of waiting for that ever-tardy Prince Charming to arrive.

Choosing the right home is driven by both qualitative and quantitative considerations and there are almost always trade-offs between the two. A garage or a garden? A finished basement or a sleeping loft? Extra bedrooms or a home office? A pool or an attached suite for the in-laws? Oh, the choices!

The primary factor for most buyers, however, is all about (you guessed it!) location, location, location. Yep, just like the real-estate agents say. As a singleton or a couple without children, you likely want to find a home close to your place of work, with easy access to your gym, movie theatres, your fabulous friends, and your favourite restaurants and clubs. Once you become parents, however, proximity to entertainment takes a back seat to good schools, quiet streets, and parks and play spaces.

 **GOLDEN RULE: THE RULE OF 32**

No, we are not talking about your dream husband's waist size. The rule of 32 gives you a measure of how much you can reasonably spend on a home. Banks, trust companies, and credit unions are generally more than happy to provide qualified purchasers with a pre-approved mortgage up to a defined amount. They calculate how much they will lend you by looking at your income and the amount of debt you carry.

Gross debt service (GDS) is a ratio of debt (i.e., principal and interest, taxes, heating, condo fees, etc.) divided by your gross monthly income and multiplied by 100. The lower the GDS ratio, the easier it will be for you to handle your debt payments. In general, a GDS of 32 per cent is usually the highest level a bank will permit. See more about this and your TDS ratio (can you guess what it means?) in the pages that follow.

## Living within Your Means: Three Easy Steps

When you're thinking of buying a house, it's important to take a hard look at what you can afford. You may *feel* like you can afford an extra

$600 a month, but when you start looking at what you can get for $800 a month, well, maybe if you cut back on going out for dinner now and then . . . but how can you be sure?

Financial advisors have invented two important ratios for taking the guesswork out of affordability. Each involves just three easy steps.

- **Gross debt service ratio**

  When it comes to housing, the rule of thumb is that your monthly housing costs should not be more than 32 per cent of your gross monthly income. Financial advisors apply a calculation known as the gross debt service ratio, or GDS (since financial types love to make acronyms out of things). It's a very simple calculation; here's how you can do it yourself:

  1. **Start with your gross monthly salary** (before deductions). If you have a hubby contributing to the payments, include his gross monthly salary as well.

  2. **Add any other monthly income you regularly receive.**

  3. **Multiply the total by 0.32.**

  The total you get is equal to your 32 per cent GDS, or the *maximum* amount you can afford to spend on monthly housing costs, including mortgage payments or rent, property taxes, and utility bills.

- **Total debt service ratio**

  To make sure you are fully living within your means, it's important to look at your *entire* monthly debt load: your total debt service ratio, or TDS. The rule of thumb here is that all of your monthly debt payments should not take up more than 40 per cent of your gross monthly income. (For you alert cookies out there, this means that you have a mere 8 per cent to work with, over and above your housing costs.) Here's how to calculate your TDS:

1. **Start with your gross monthly salary** (before deductions). If you're including your hubby's debts in the exercise, include his gross monthly salary as well.

2. **Add any other monthly income you regularly receive.**

3. **Multiply the total by 0.40.**

The total you get is equal to your 40 per cent TDS, or the *maximum* amount you can afford to spend on your housing costs, your car payments, and all the other credit payments you make each month, including any additional mortgages, leases, credit cards (yes, those too!), lines of credit, student loans, and other personal loans.

If you find you actually spend less on housing than your GDS calculation, and less on debt payments than your TDS calculation, then congratulations, frugal girl! Technically, you are living within your means. Just remember, those are your *upper* limits. The lower you keep your ratios, the more disposable income you will have to enjoy each month. What you choose to do with that disposable income, and whether or not your spending remains within the limits of that income, may be another story.

## The Lowdown on Down Payments

When it comes to down payments, bigger is always better. If you can't afford to save a good-sized down payment (about 10 to 20 per cent of the cost of the house), chances are you won't be able to afford saving for emergencies or the future once you are in that house. Real estate always comes with a myriad of hidden costs, from repairs to unexpected structural issues, and the problem of "uninvited guests" (i.e., *critters*, not relatives!). So it's essential to consider the whole picture and be prepared.

Saving for a down payment can also make you think more carefully about how much you want to spend (or rather, *should* spend). When the difference between a $365,000 and a $400,000 home means saving an extra $7,000 for the down payment, you might just start to question how badly you want whatever comes with that more expensive house. Requiring a larger down payment can also mean having to delay your purchase in order to save the additional funds, which could get in the way of apartment-lease end dates, real-estate-market conditions, and passing up that lovely, but slightly smaller house you've been eyeing. What to do? Think through the implications and make the best choice that you can, given the situation.

## Mortgages: Terms and Meanings

- **Term:** The length of time that the mortgage agreement stays in force. This generally ranges from six months to seven years.

- **Amortization:** The length of time needed to pay off the mortgage in full. Most first-time buyers choose a 25-year amortization. Shortening your amortization period will decrease the total interest you pay, but it means your monthly payments against the principal will increase.

- **Frequency:** You can generally choose from monthly, semi-monthly, weekly, biweekly, or accelerated weekly/biweekly. Choosing an accelerated payment schedule means that you make the equivalent of an extra month's payment over the course of the year. Over the long term, this will decrease your interest costs and help you to be mortgage-free sooner.

- **Open or closed?:** An open mortgage can be paid off at any time without penalty. A closed mortgage means that you're locked in until the end of your term. If you want to pay it off ahead of schedule, there will be a penalty.

## More Than Just a Pretty Rate

When you begin shopping for a mortgage, you enter the world of rate competition. Every bank and lending company hopes to entice you by dangling shiny low lending rates before your eyes. Do not be easily swayed by all the glittery mortgage glam. Rates are important, but they are not the whole story. When choosing a mortgage, the two most important factors are:

1. **the amount of interest** that you will pay over the full term of the mortgage (*hint: less is more!*); and

2. **the balance owing when the mortgage expires** and you become exposed to new rates.

Here's the thing: rates can fluctuate with economic conditions, which are generally out of your control. So although you might enjoy a relatively low rate for two years, the renewal rate at the end of the term could be significantly higher. Compare this to locking in at a moderate rate for five years and having better rate stability for a longer period of time.

Similarly, while a closed mortgage with a fixed rate for three years might seem like a safe bet, an open mortgage with a variable rate could be even more advantageous for you, if you structure your cash flow in such a way that you can pay down your principal quickly. Variable mortgages might also allow you to lock in at a particular rate at some point over the term, which can help to mitigate risk if rates start to rise.

If you are starting to feel your head spin, you're not alone. Trying to figure out whether interest rates will rise or fall (and when!) is difficult for economists and analysts who follow the markets on a full-time basis, let alone potential borrowers. When you are in the market for a mortgage, pay attention to what analysts and economists are saying about the future of interest rates, ask lots of questions, and seek out information where you can (financial institutions and real-estate resources can be good places to start). You also have to listen to that little voice inside of you, the one that lets you know if you are comfortable or uncomfortable, and make the best decision you can.

Remember, you don't *have* to buy that bigger house right now. If the mere thought makes that little voice scream "no," chances are you can find your comfort zone elsewhere and move forward.

A smart girl knows that bargain rates are no bargain if they mean that you are locked into a situation that doesn't allow you to pay down the mortgage quickly. Limiting your ability to make extra payments is bad for you and good for the lender. Your goal is to avoid paying excess interest and the way you do that is not by locking into a low-rate mortgage forever (thereby, guaranteeing a big chunk of interest paid over the term). Rather, you need to focus on rapidly reducing the principal upon which that interest is calculated.

## The Takeaway

Be wary of those pretty little rates and focus on the total amount of interest you will be expected to pay for the duration of the mortgage. Look for every opportunity you can to pay down the mortgage, such as making biweekly payments (rather than monthly), annual opportunities to apply a lump-sum payment without any fee penalties, and the chance to increase your mortgage payments at some point down the road. For more details, see below!

## Tips for Paying Off Your Mortgage Faster

✓ **Reduce your amortization:** Amortization is the length of time needed to reduce the balance to zero. A shorter amortization means that your regular payments will be higher, but you'll reduce your total interest costs and own your home, mortgage-free, much sooner.

✓ **Switch from monthly to an accelerated weekly or biweekly payment schedule:** With an accelerated payment schedule, you make the equivalent of one extra month's payment every year. This reduces your total interest cost and helps you to pay down your principal more quickly.

The savings can be significant. For example, on a $200,000 mortgage at 4.5 per cent amortized over 25 years, switching from monthly payments to an accelerated weekly schedule will save you more than $20,000 in interest over the life of the mortgage and reduce your amortization by almost three years.

✓ **Take advantage of prepayment options:** Most lenders will allow you to increase your regular payment up to 100 per cent without penalty. The extra money goes directly to the principal. In addition, most lenders will allow you to prepay a certain percentage of the original mortgage amount on each anniversary.

✓ **At renewal time, pay down as much as possible:** When you renew, you're generally allowed to pay down as much of the mortgage principal as you want without penalty. Take advantage of this opportunity!

---

 **DID YOU KNOW? TURNING OFF THE METER**

Say you have a $100,000 mortgage with a 7 per cent interest rate per year. If you pay it off in 15 years, rather than over 25 years, your monthly payments will be nearly $200 more, yet you will save nearly $50,000 in interest. Now, that's some serious cash!

---

## The Cost of Bells and Whistles

Congratulations, you're pre-approved for a mortgage and now you know the price range within which you can shop (*likely more money than you've ever spent in your life!*). However, it's important to carefully consider *all* of the costs before you start falling in love with houses at the top end of that range. You may very well need a buffer zone of cash to cover the litany of new-home-related expenses.

Let's consider a few of those sneaky items that can shrink your shopping budget:

- **Moving costs**

  Moving from one home to another involves numerous costs, such as:

  - ✓ movers (your pals—beer and pizza; movers—a couple thousand dollars);
  - ✓ legal costs (another thousand or two);
  - ✓ appraisals (typically a few hundred or more);
  - ✓ taxes (e.g., land-transfer tax—approximately 1–2 per cent of the total property value);
  - ✓ mortgage-restructuring costs; and
  - ✓ potential penalties (i.e., if you are leaving your apartment before the end of the term or transferring a mortgage).

  It's important to factor in these not-so-nominal costs (i.e., we're talking *thousands* of dollars) to ensure that you are not left with an empty bank account on moving day.

- **Furnishing and decorating**

  These costs can really add up and may include items you need to consider purchasing before you move in, such as painting, flooring, appliances, and window coverings. Purchasing additional furniture to fill up all those new rooms can be offset by selling some of your older pieces that are no longer needed or do not fit into your new decor (hello, on-line classified ads!).

  When it comes to cosmetic updates, pick and choose the overhauls that will make the most impact, and be selective! Sometimes just updating the light fixtures and hardware in a kitchen can mean leaving the cupboards aside (for now, at least). You don't need to do *everything* all at once (even though the urge feels insurmountable).

- **Repairs and maintenance**

  With the joys of home ownership comes the responsibility for upkeep and repairs. (Why is it that problems always happen when we least expect them? Like on a Sunday, when repair services are at a minimum and cost is at a maximum?) The older the property, the more often you will be faced with breakdowns and maintenance work, so plan to have emergency funds on hand. This may require you to spend less on the purchase price and put the balance of your mortgage funds into an emergency savings account. (When your water heater blows and the air conditioner is on the blink, you will be glad you did!)

- **The real bells and whistles**

  Newly built properties can be a money trap of a different kind. The original price can rapidly escalate, as you are offered seemingly endless upgrades, such as tiles, appliances, lighting, cabinetry, carpets, and a host of others. Individually, the upgrades may not seem too costly, but add them together and . . . *what?!* Remember, you don't need to upgrade everything immediately. As much as you love hardwood flooring, you could live with the standard carpeting until it wears out and then make the change. The other thing to consider is if you can find your own contractors at some point in the future and do the upgrades for less.

---

 **HINDSIGHT**

*When I first walked into my new house, I had all kinds of ideas of changes I would make: knock out a wall here; change up a paint colour there; install some fabulous, dramatic window coverings. I didn't do those things off*

*(continued)*

> *the hop, probably due to not wanting to incur the extra costs so soon after*
> *making a major purchase, and am I ever glad that I didn't.*
>
> *Instead, I got a chance to live in the house, to experience where the light*
> *fell, why certain things had been designed as they were, what the place*
> *was really about. I did make changes down the road, but not any of*
> *the changes that I originally thought I would. By giving the house a*
> *chance to reveal itself to me and help me understand it, I was able to*
> *save money and make the adjustments that really showed off my home*
> *in its best light.*

## The R-Word: Renovations

Admit it, you're addicted. From drooling over *Architectural Digest*, to perusing design blogs, to PVR-ing all those kooky and often tacky reality-television home-makeover shows, your imagination gets fired up with just a voyeuristic glimpse into the way other people live. Like those weight-loss losers of the biggest kind, the thrill is in bearing witness to the power of transformation, in this case, of the home. ("I never would have thought of using aubergine in the kitchen. Could my bathroom really look that great, too? And in one *afternoon!*")

Home makeovers are especially tantalizing and inspiring in their promise of transforming your home with a coat of paint, some new throw pillows, and *er*, just knocking out a wall here and there (have sledgehammer, will mesmerize!). The proliferation of DIY guides and programs makes home projects and renovations seem within reach, even on the smallest of budgets. And yet, you know in your heart that once you get started, these projects have a way of getting *way* out of hand (some designers refer to it as "project creep" or the "why not?" scenario). Whatever you call it, big dollars always seem to follow.

But here's the catch: renovations on their own are not bad things. After all, don't real-estate professionals always tell us that they increase the value of our homes and our investment? Well, yes, but it depends how much borrowing and leveraging a girl needs to do to get her dream kitchen. The key is to keep the process manageable, develop an overall vision, and stick with it. Here are a few tips for helping you keep smart renovations within reach:

- **Set priorities**

  Identify the most pressing projects in your home and choose one manageable project at a time—something that will make the most positive difference in your family's day-to-day life and where you will reap the most rewards. As the story goes, kitchens and bathrooms generally retain their value if done well and are good investments (and selling features), so consider these important hubs when setting renovation priorities.

- **DIY or find a contractor**

  Ask yourself if this is the type of renovation project that you can do yourself, such as painting or basic landscaping, or whether specialized renovation assistance is required. In some cases, such as replacing flooring, you can save money by tearing out the existing carpet yourself (not glamorous, but totally doable) and having the new hardwood floors installed by a professional.

- **Look for reasonable learning opportunities**

  Just because you haven't tried a particular renovation project before, such as replacing a kitchen faucet, doesn't mean you can't learn how to do it yourself. There is an abundance of how-to books, websites, clinics at your local home-improvement retailer, and even videos on-line. The key is to choose a small project, study the resources, and get started. You will be amazed by how good you will feel, how quickly your competency will increase, and how much money you will save by doing it yourself. This is true get-*her*-done, girl attitude!

· **Price and budget for the job**

Depending on the nature of the project, you can either price out the job yourself (if it's a small project) or seek pricing quotes from qualified contractors or service providers. It's a good idea to get two or three quotes and make sure to use only qualified contractors (friends can provide referrals, and make sure to check contractor references). Pricing should include materials, labour, and any other cost components. When setting a budget, build in a contingency of 10 to 15 per cent for any unanticipated items and stick with your budget.

· **Manage the debt**

To keep your debt in check, pay down your existing debt, ideally in the amount of *double* your renovation budget. *Hey, what?* We know, this is the hard part, but it's this step that will make all the difference to your finances. For example, if you want to redo your bathroom at an expense of $5,000, first pay down your debt by $10,000.

· **Monitor, monitor, monitor**

Once the project gets going, it can be easy to get distracted. If it's a DIY, your eye might start to wander to the weekend sunshine (wouldn't an afternoon on the deck be great?). If you have a contractor working on the project, you might start to notice that the workdays are getting shorter and less frequent. As with many projects, they often start with lots of enthusiasm and then start to fade. The key here is to keep your eye on the prize and monitor the progress of the project to keep it moving forward. After all, you don't want to be stepping over paint cans and brushes forever, do you? As the homeowner, it's up to you to keep it moving.

## The Takeaway

Balance, focus on your overall plan, and recognize that you don't have to do everything all at once. Just have that second cup of coffee and enjoy the process!

 **GOLDEN RULE: LIVE WITHIN YOUR NEIGHBOURHOOD**

Before you turn your perfectly acceptable new home into the most outstanding home on the block, consider the location and the value of the homes around you. If you go for every upgrade or high-end renovation and then need to sell your home for an unforeseen reason, the price you will want to recover may be significantly higher than the average selling price within your neighbourhood. This can make it tough to sell, and even tougher to recoup your investment. Keep up with the Joneses if you must, but recognize that there is limited payoff in *outdoing* the Joneses.

## Home Couture Comes at a Cost

Now let's pretend you've lived in your home, given it some time, and let the required renovations speak to you. And now you're ready to thoroughly gut the kitchen! If you're like most of us, you're probably dreaming of something that your very-real savings won't cover. And if that's the case, now is the time to explore your financing options. (Just please do so after consulting with your financial planner: going into serious debt just to have design-magazine-worthy drama is *so* not worth it.)

Here are three financing options to consider:

**1. Use a home-equity line of credit**

A line of credit gives you access to a predetermined amount of credit on demand. Generally, you can borrow up to 75 per cent of the appraised value of your home, or up to 90 per cent if the line of credit is insured.

There are some real pluses to going with this option, including:

- ease and convenience. You may have the option of writing cheques or using a credit or bank card;
- you can take what you need, when you need it, and pay interest only on the outstanding amount;
- a line of credit secured against the value of your house will typically be issued at a lower rate than an unsecured loan or personal line of credit; and
- flexible repayment. You can pay some or all of the outstanding balance at any time without penalty, or make interest-only payments.

## 2. Increase your existing mortgage

You also have the option of increasing the amount of your mortgage to help finance your renovation. This option is ideal if:

- your mortgage is coming due;
- you're selling one house to buy another;
- you're taking out your first mortgage; or
- you're locked into a long-term mortgage at a significantly higher rate than is currently available. In this case, the savings in interest over the long term could offset any penalty you may incur for restructuring the mortgage.

This option isn't as flexible as a line of credit, but it does offer some advantages:

- the borrowed funds are structured to be paid back in a set amount of time; and
- interest rates can be fixed, if you choose—unlike a line of credit, which floats against prime.

### 3. Get a second mortgage

A second mortgage is just that: a mortgage that is in addition to your first mortgage. Like a first mortgage, a second mortgage is a loan with a specified rate of interest and repayment schedule.

A second mortgage can be a good choice if you are locked into a long-term mortgage, but wouldn't benefit from breaking your first mortgage. Do note, however, that lending rates for a second mortgage are generally higher than those for a first mortgage.

Like increasing your mortgage, this option trades repayment flexibility for the peace of mind of knowing the debt will be paid down if you stick to the repayment schedule.

## The Takeaway

Yes, renovations are exciting. But stay focused on the big (financial) picture, smart girl.

As many of us know, things can quickly get out of hand. If you are using a home-equity line of credit or mortgage funding, it should be used for the purpose of adding *value* to the home through renovations or invested in other assets that appreciate over time. Access to this credit shouldn't be used for depreciating consumer items such as TVs for every room, cars to fill that oversized garage, and so on.

Above all else, the biggest downside, regardless of which financing option you choose, is that you are adding more debt to your balance sheet. You must be cautious not to put yourself in a situation where you have too much debt that is tax inefficient (i.e., not deductible against income). Therefore, as tempting as a massive design overhaul may seem, always remain cautious about the amount borrowed and be careful to balance that with the value, appreciation, and enjoyment you will get in return. This balanced approach is the key to creating wealth over the long term.

As with anything, seek trusted professional financial advice before doing anything that significantly impacts your balance sheet!

---

 **LIFE LESSON: LOVE THE HOME YOU'RE IN**

No home can ever be perfect, so decide on the compromises you can live with and learn to love them as a whole. Once you own it and make it yours, your home will have a magical way of endearing itself to you (and it just might surprise you how much). Despite the little creaks or areas you thought you must change *immediately*, you might find many unexpected advantages or conveniences that will make you wonder how you ever lived without them.

It is tempting to focus on what still needs to be done, but it's important to recognize that your home will evolve over time, reflecting your experiences, your changing design tastes (and they really do change), your family's growth, and, of course, your budget. The most beautiful and comfortable homes we've ever been inside were not filled with sumptuously decorated, magazine-perfect rooms, but rather, had started out bare and the owners slowly collected furnishings, making gradual adjustments and additions over time. These are the houses that really are *homes*, expressing the genuine warmth, pleasures, and values of their owners.

Concentrate on making your home a place where you, your family, and your guests feel happy and welcome, rather than seeking to impress with a showroom ideal (how boring!).

---

## Your Vehicle

It's a little-known fact that in the world of auto buying, women hold a lot of power—purchasing power, that is. According to *Road & Travel Magazine*, 65 per cent of all new cars and 53 per cent of used cars in the United States are purchased by women. According to the same study, women influence 95 per cent of all auto purchases. Wow! Who knew?

And we're not just talking about the variety of cars that get you from point A to point B. Luxury cars, long the domain of men with James Bond aspirations (or complexes), are rising in popularity as a spending priority for women. In China, where female millionaires are being minted faster than anywhere else in the world, luxury-car sales are skyrocketing. Thirty per cent of Maserati's sales in China are to women, as compared to only 10 per cent in Europe. Ferrari claims that women account for 20 per cent of their sales in China, twice their typical average.

No matter what type of vehicle you buy, there is a key consideration: while a home is generally an *appreciating* asset that will increase in value over time (assuming, of course, that you maintain and take good care of it), a car is definitely a *depreciating* asset (unless it has some vintage-collector value). By depreciating, we mean that every year it's worth less and less until the value eventually becomes nominal over time.

Yet the vast majority of people do not focus on the value of the vehicle they buy, nor even the total purchase price. Most car buyers consider one thing only: the monthly payment. In truthing, focusing on this alone, you can use a little creativity and negotiating power to make almost any car fit into your monthly budget. Yet focusing on the monthly payment alone and not the overall cost of the vehicle is one of the all-time most common—and expensive—mistakes that purchasers make.

---

 **GOLDEN RULE: THE THREE-YEAR RULE**

Always choose a vehicle and a payment plan that allow you to pay off the car within 36 months. Three years and no more! If this means you can't afford the monthly payments, then you can't afford the car.

*(continued)*

> The same rule applies to leasing: select a car that you could afford to fully purchase within 36 months. Bank the difference between the lease payment and the would-be loan payment and you will even save yourself a bit of money over the term.

## Car-to-Home Ratio

Here's another way to put your car purchase in perspective: think about what you spend on your (depreciating) car compared to what you spend on your (appreciating) home.

If, for example, you are making car payments of $1,200 per month (for one or maybe two vehicles), while making mortgage payments of $1,800 per month, then you are paying *two-thirds* of your mortgage cost on your vehicles. Clearly, this is not a choice that makes good financial sense.

Put another way, suppose your family has a $42,000 SUV and a $52,000 car. If your home is valued at $376,000, then your expenditure on vehicles represents roughly a quarter of the value of your home! Not to mention the cost of gas, maintenance, and insurance. That's a lot of money!

What's a more appropriate level? Whatever car you can comfortably purchase in full within 3 years. See the connection? Since the average car is on the road for 8.5 years, this will give you plenty of time to save for a new one. Over time, you will be able to make larger down payments, with the ultimate goal of paying cash for your car purchase and avoiding interest payments altogether. Now, that's a sensible approach.

 **GOLDEN RULE: LEASING FOR BUSINESS OWNERS**

Be careful! Leasing makes it easier to drive away in a car that is more expensive than you could afford to buy. And here's the rub: you are

*(continued)*

making monthly payments on a car that is depreciating in value, while still being on the hook for its *original* value, and not even owning it in the end. That's triple trouble!

The financially prudent thing to do is to stick to our Three-Year Golden Rule and only lease a car that you could afford to buy outright over 36 months. Used in this way, leasing a vehicle can be an economically ideal option for business owners, but *only* if you have the legitimate ability to write off at least 50 per cent of the lease payments for tax purposes.

## Your Vacation Property

For many families, a vacation property is an idyllic refuge. The beach, the lake, the mountains; this is a place to make memories that will last forever, where the stresses of daily life drift away on the tide, and where a family can relax, have fun, and renew their bond with one another.

There is no question that a vacation property can deliver fantastic intangible returns. But, is it a wise investment? And if not, what are your options?

While many families share long histories of oceanside or lakeside properties, many choose to rent or visit resorts, rather than buying their own vacation property. Family traditions are made by returning to the same spot year after year (and this doesn't necessarily mean owning it). By renting or staying at a resort, a family can enjoy the same kind of vacation togetherness for a fraction of the cost (and a fraction of the headache) of ownership.

Before you start shopping for a cottage or vacation property, do yourself a favour and do a little math:

- **Step 1: Quantify the potential usage**

  How many weeks in the average year will you be able to use the cottage? Don't be theoretical; use this year as an example.

Don't forget to factor in the reality check of the weather in your area (boating to your island cottage past October could be just a little on the frozen side and driving on ice will definitely not be a safe option at certain times, either).

- **Step 2: Get pricing information**

  Collect information about the price of a cottage or property you would like, based on comparable prices in your ideal location. Remember that the low end of the price range can be "handyman-special" properties, so assuming that you want indoor plumbing, be realistic and consider the middle of the price range as a general starting point.

- **Step 3: Understand the costs (and potential revenue opportunities)**

  Develop a rough estimate of the annual operating costs, including the mortgage payments, property taxes, utilities, insurance (including health insurance if you're crossing borders), transportation costs, and upkeep. Consider if you will require a caretaker to look in on the property when you are not there, as some insurance policies require at least periodic visits to the property. On the flip side, could you generate any income from renting out your property? Be realistic, in terms of what it would take to find qualified renters (make your place a "no-keg zone"), the implications of renting (it's 2 a.m., the indoor plumbing is plugged, and you are two hours away!), and any additional costs, such as renter-friendly insurance policies.

- **Step 4: Understand the costs to rent (your own costs, that is)**

  Check out the price of cottage or property rentals in your ideal location and figure out how much it would cost to rent a similar vacation property for the same number of weeks as in Step 1. Be realistic about what it will cost to rent a property that will comfortably meet your needs.

Now, tally up the numbers and compare: are you better off renting or are you really ready to buy? You might find that the best approach is to continue to rent, until perhaps increased work flexibility would allow you to spend enough time at your retreat to justify a purchase. Think of it this way: you could use your rental years as a means to do first-hand market research, to find out exactly where you would like to be when you are ready to purchase.

 **A LAWYER'S TAKE ON MAJOR PURCHASES**

An individual's personal and financial situation will be key factors when considering purchasing items such as a home, a car, or a second home. Here are some things to consider:

- **Marital property legislation** (which differs from jurisdiction to jurisdiction) will dictate how such items are to be shared in the event of marital breakdown and, in many cases, death. Pre-nuptial agreements can look after some of these factors.

- **Tax considerations** are also important. For instance, purchasing vacation property in another jurisdiction can open up the taxpayer to potentially paying estate taxes in the jurisdiction of the vacation property, *as well as* in the taxpayer's jurisdiction of residence.

- In some cases, depending upon a person's circumstances, legal and accounting professionals may recommend purchasing the property via a **vacation trust resident in the taxpayer's province in Canada, so as to avoid estate taxes in the United States** (for Canadians acquiring vacation property in the States). This decision will depend on, among other things, the taxpayer's total portfolio of assets. Talk to your advisor(s) for further details and explanation.

## Keeping It in the Family

If you are fortunate to have a cottage already in your family, you know how precious it is and how tricky it can be when it comes to succession planning. When several children and their families share an emotional attachment, as well as a desire to maintain the cottage, careful financial planning is key.

Here are some approaches to keep in mind:

- **Tax considerations**

  Depending where you live, a principal residence may be exempt from capital gains and other tax implications. This means, for example, that if the cottage is sold or transferred to someone in the family for whom it can be deemed as a principal residence, you may be able to transfer the property tax-free.

- **Gifting a property**

  This approach won't get you out of the tax implications, but it is important not to "sell" the cottage to a family member for a dollar or a nominal amount, since that price will become the cost base for the next sale. If it's transferred as a gift for zero consideration, then the cost base for any future sale would be based on fair market value at the time the gift was transferred.

- **Life insurance to cover the taxes**

  If the property will not be transferred until the current owner dies, the easiest way to ensure cash is available to pay the taxes is through a life-insurance policy. Explore the options and plan accordingly.

- **Trust accounts or a corporation**

  Another option is to transfer the cottage into a trust account with the heirs as beneficiaries, or a corporation where the heirs hold the shares. This allows the property to be held consistently throughout generations of family members. The beneficiaries of the trust or shareholders must plan ahead to ensure a smooth transfer of their interests upon each of their deaths.

## The Takeaway

Given the various approaches and parties involved, a good approach is to seek specialized advice in this area to understand the options and choose the approach that is best for you and your family. Not only can it save you unexpected tax costs, it can also help to keep peace in the family for the long term.

---

 **HINDSIGHT**

*My clients came to me and said they wanted to buy a cottage. Though they have high incomes, they already held a mortgage of over $300,000 and were not making progress on reducing their existing debt. They felt that, given their salaries, they "ought" to be able to afford a cottage. Both of them worked long hours to keep their incomes up, so they certainly felt they needed a cottage.*

*We figured out that the annual costs on the cottage they wanted to buy would be upwards of $10,000. Yet, their cash-flow situation allowed them only about $5,000 a year. Meanwhile, four weeks of a similar cottage rental in the area they chose would cost only $2,000. In the end, we came up with a spending plan that allowed one of them to reduce their working hours by 20 per cent.*

*Even with this change, their financial plan remained on track. They realized that what they really craved was more leisure time and that they were merely channelling that into the idea of owning a cottage.*

## Your Investment Property

Buying a property for investment purposes can be fabulous or fright-ful; there's often no in-between! Not only are you vulnerable to tenant concerns (and headaches!), but to market cycles as well.

If you are a newbie to owning a rental property, an owner-occu-pied property is a good way to go. This means that you purchase an income property where you actually live on the premises. You have plenty of options: an owner-occupied property can include anything from a home with a basement apartment, to a multi-unit apartment complex. You will likely have more advantageous lending options, since banks consider you less of a risk if you are willing to live in the property (and therefore handle those middle-of-the-night emergen-cies yourself—fun!).

Should you decide to take the investment-property plunge, here are our top three must-dos:

1. **DO start small, by purchasing a property that you can main-tain in the event that you are without a tenant for a few months.** If you are totally dependent on rental income, you might find yourself in a bind if you lose that rent for a month or two, particularly in the early days of ownership.

2. **DO think of your investment property as a tool to build net worth rather than to generate income, at least for the first few years.** Once you've paid some of the mortgage down and you've got a cash cushion, then and only then can you start to feel comfortable using some of the income. Slow and steady wins the race!

3. **DO be cautious of how much you are borrowing to buy an investment property.** Your GDS can be driven up and reduce your ability to borrow in the future. Keep in mind that banks don't typically allow you to use 100 per cent of the

property-rental income in determining *your* income, as they also realize that tenants come and go.

Once you have the chance to gain some experience with investment properties, you will be in a much better position to determine whether you want to buy, hold, or fold. This approach is a winner either way, as it facilitates slow and steady growth or an easier exit.

---

 **HINDSIGHT**

*I owned a rental property once. Today, if you asked me if I'd prefer to invest in a rental property or get shot in the foot, I would choose being shot in the foot because it would heal faster.*

*Many people don't realize how much responsibility and expense they are biting off with these things until they are choking on it. Property-buying television shows make it seem like you buy a rental property and then turn on the money tap. The risks are very under-played and the liabilities can create huge consequences. I'm not saying don't ever do it, I'm just saying think through every outcome and make sure you are fully ready for the responsibilities you're get-ting yourself into.*

---

## Know When to Fold 'Em

Perhaps the only thing tougher than making the decision to *buy* a major purchase is making the decision as to when to *sell* it. Over the years, you will have put an immense amount of time, money, and energy into buying and maintaining your house, car, or cottage. When it comes to selling, emotions can cloud your judgment every bit as much as when you were on the buying end.

Investment advisors recommend having a *sell discipline* when it comes to investing in the stock market. This is a strategy that helps advisors to understand their clients' objectives so they can determine when it's appropriate to sell an investment.

What's your sell discipline with respect to your major purchases, and what are the signs that you need to look out for? How do you know when the time is right to just let go?

- **Recall the original plan**

  Think back to the beginning. When you first made the acquisition, what was your goal? Was it a certain increase in value? Was there a purpose that has now been fulfilled? It's perfectly fine and natural to re-evaluate and extend your original plan, but on the other hand, perhaps you've achieved what you set out to do and now it's time to move on.

- **Accept any sunk costs**

  If you find that you are in the unfortunate position of having paid too much for an investment that is just not paying off, swallow your pride and cut your losses. You can't reverse the costs you've sunk, so accept the price you've paid and pay no more.

- **Base your next success on this experience**

  Learn from your wins and your losses and evaluate what you would do better next time around. Don't let life's lessons make you cynical. Optimists have way more fun.

Just as a sell discipline can indicate when it's time to get out gracefully, it can also guide you toward staying invested. When things aren't going particularly well, fear and panic might make you consider getting out of an investment prematurely. A strategy that defines and reminds you of your criteria for selling can put things back in perspective and help you to keep the faith.

**LIFE LESSON: WHEN LIFE TAKES AN UNEXPECTED TURN**

When life happens and things don't go as planned, an asset, such as a home or cottage, may have to be sold. Depending on the circumstances, this might be really sad or a big relief. In financial terms, however, while real estate tends to appreciate in value over time, in nearly every market, there are periods of low or negative growth. In the case of a sudden setback, whether death, disability, or divorce (or simply realizing you made a mistake and need to unwind it for sanity's sake), it is possible that you may have to divest of a property at a loss. If this property is your principal residence, the loss will probably not be tax deductible (depending where you live).

The emotional consequences of selling the family home, for example, can be more stressful than any financial loss or gain. It is sometimes necessary to take a reality check and realize that your family is still a family, even if you have to make an unforeseen move.

As a parent, your instinct is to shelter your children in times of crisis, but to do so at the risk of financial peril is shortsighted. Children are more resilient than we think, particularly when they are assured of the continuity of their parents' love. Ask yourself if clinging to the family home is possibly more about your own needs, rather than "for the sake of the children." Financial stability is more important than the continuity of one particular roof. If moving and downsizing can help to stabilize your financial situation and reduce overwhelming stress, then you will be doing the very best to keep your family safe and protected.

# 7

## Making Your Money Work For You

### *Finance and Investing*

### You Work Hard for Your Money

You've *earned* it. How good do those words feel? Whether it's buying yourself a special treat, indulging in a glass of wine with dinner, or simply taking time out to sit in the sun and indulge in a gossip rag, being rewarded for your hard work, intellect, and talent is incredibly gratifying, isn't it?

And when you earn an income, that payday feeling is not just about the money. Think of it as a reminder that your efforts and contributions are recognized and valued. And while you may have long forgotten the satisfaction of your first job, making money of your own goes a long way to boosting confidence and self-worth.

All this positive talk aside, if you've been in the workforce for a while, at some point you may find yourself wondering: "Hello! When is this going to *really* pay off?" As in, no matter how many hours you work, how many accolades you receive, or how many raises or bonuses you get—do you still find yourself living paycheque to (meagre) paycheque? What's left at the end of the month, beyond a knot in your stomach and a profound gratitude for over-draft protection?

Yes, sometimes it can feel like you're just working to live and living to work ("I mean c'mon, will I *ever* get ahead?"). Fear not, friend. You're certainly not alone and you have every right to start questioning this whole working-for-a-living thing.

Indeed, if you feel like you're on a never-ending treadmill of earn-ing and bill paying, then it's time to think about how your money can start working *for you*. Because guess what, it really *can*!

## Get-Rich-Slow Scheme

Believe it or not, that money you earn can be used to earn *more* money, if you let it. No, we're not talking about some get-rich-quick scheme. (Those are for smooth, sweet-talkers, and the fools who fol-low, neither of which describes you.)

We're talking about leaving the treadmill at the gym (or hidden under a pile of clothes in your bedroom) and getting yourself properly *invested* in order to seriously build your long-term earning power. And that starts with the basics.

"Investing" refers to the exchange of capital (money) for a level of partial or full ownership in something that is expected to deliver a financial return or profit to the investor. Before making an investment, smart investors engage in thorough research and analysis.

Now, people who invest money without proper research and analysis are called "speculators." They are less interested in the qual-ity or long-term viability of their investment, so long as it delivers a quick profit.

Investing versus speculating is kind of like a health-and-fitness regime versus a crash diet. If you want to lose weight, a plan that incorporates a balanced diet, regular exercise, and causes you to lose weight slowly over time will have a much more lasting effect on your waistline than one that forces you to eat nothing but cabbage soup for two weeks.

Forget the quick fix. To build wealth for a lifetime, proper investing requires patience and discipline to stick with the strategy, bit by bit, day after day. You can expect moderate, incremental, and long-lasting results that add up to big successes over time. Be the turtle, not the hare, honey.

Sounds simple, right? In its essence, it kind of is. Yet for many of us, investments, the markets, and the world of finance can seem incredibly intimidating—what with all the charts, numbers, and terminology that seem designed to appeal only to those with an economics degree (and we know how much most of us loved *that* class).

But here's a secret: the world of investments is kind of like the world of technology. Despite the fact that you may not know your ASCII from your DOS, you still manage to use a computer every day. (How could you live without it?)

In fact, the icon of the investment world, legendary stock-market investor and billionaire tycoon Warren Buffett has said, "To invest successfully over a lifetime does not require a stratospheric IQ, unusual business insights or inside information. What's needed is a sound intellectual framework for making decisions and the ability to keep emotions from corroding that framework."[1]

Uh-huh. Two problems with that, right?

1. How do I go about getting myself "a sound intellectual framework for making decisions"?

   and . . .

2. "Keep [my] emotions from corroding that framework"? *As if!*

---

[1] Benjamin Graham, Warren Buffett, and Jason Zweig, *The Intelligent Investor: The Definitive Book on Value Investing*, Rev Edition (New York: Harper Paperbacks, 2003).

As women, we might consider ourselves to be highly emotional beings (or at least, that's the stereotype). Men are the ones who are more decisive and therefore better at investing, right? *Au contraire, ma chérie.* Studies show that when it comes to investing, women do more upfront research, spend more time selecting companies, are more likely to invest in companies they understand, hold onto shares longer, and generally take fewer risks than men.[2]

In 2010, Vanguard, a mutual fund company, released the results of a two-year study of 2.7 million investors, which was conducted during the thick of the global financial market meltdown. They found that men were 10 per cent more likely to panic and sell when prices were at the bottom of the market. (Talk about emotional!) Women, on the other hand, were more likely to stick to the investments they made, through thick and thin.[3]

It turns out that men are often *overconfident* in their abilities to time the market and make smart investment decisions. As a result, they trade their stocks more frequently and end up paying a lot more in trading fees. Women, on the other hand, tend to be more anxious about making a wrong decision, are more likely to admit what they don't know, and, in the face of uncertainty, will often delay making a decision.[4]

So perhaps our emotions *don't* always get in the way of good judgment. Perhaps, when it comes to investing, those self-doubting womanly neuroses are actually working *in our favour*! Hmmm . . .

Warren Buffett of the buy-and-hold doctrine would certainly think so. As would Philip Fisher (may he rest in peace), another fantastically successful stock-market investor who famously said,

---

[2] GoldenGirlFinance.ca, "Invest Like a Girl, Warren Buffett Does!" 19 June 2011, http://www.goldengirlfinance.ca/articles/investing/invest-like-a-girl-warren-buffett-does
[3] Sue Shellenbarger, "In Recessions, Do Women Have Investment Edge?" *The Juggle* (blog), *Wall Street Journal*, 19 March 2010, http://blogs.wsj.com/juggle/2010/03/19/in-recessions-do-women-have-investment-edge/
[4] LouAnn Lofton, *Warren Buffett Invests Like A Girl* (New York: Collins Business, 2011).

"If the job has been correctly done when a common stock is purchased, the time to sell it is almost never."[5]

You see, once you start investing (slowly, carefully, and a little at a time), you will be amazed at how good it feels to see your little nest egg grow (and grow, and grow). The effects of compound interest, investment returns, and dividends can make your savings multiply, kind of like free money. It's a beautiful thing.

Think of it this way: there are only so many hours in a day in which you can work to earn money. But when you get your *money* earning money for *you*, well, that's when things really start to roll.

## The Sound Intellectual Framework

Oh, Mr. Buffett, you're killing us with the cryptic talk! Sound intellectual framework?

All this means is that you need to know what you want to get out of your investments. It means that when you make an investment in a company, you have an idea of what you anticipate the investment will do, how long you intend to hold it, and what kind of return you expect over your time frame.

Yes, there will be ups and downs (inherent in stock-market investing), but by staying focused on your plan (the sound intellectual framework by which you make decisions), you are more likely to have a clear head to assess when you've achieved your goal and it's time to sell; or when you need to cut your losses; or when it's wiser to hold on and ride out the inevitable bumps because you have faith in the long term. Kind of works for most things in life (*ahem*, relationships), no?

You will have many different types of investments throughout your life: your car, your home, your retirement portfolio, and your

---

[5] Philip A. Fisher, *Common Stocks and Uncommon Profits and Other Writings* (Hoboken, NJ: Wiley, 2003), p. 85.

savings plans (throw a fabulous piece of art and a little gold into the mix, too). And then there are your securities. Yes, your investments in securities (e.g., stocks, bonds, and mutual funds) may be held within a government-registered retirement portfolio or as a separate investment portfolio, or both.

The point is, however you choose to hold your securities, the key to structuring a fabulous portfolio is to take a layered approach. Yes, *layered*. You know, the way you might throw on a silk camisole, a cotton shirt, and a cashmere sweater (and maybe a chic scarf, *why not?*) as you head out for the day, not knowing exactly how the weather will behave or how much air conditioning you might face. Layering means you will be comfortable and prepared for anything: rain, wind, or investment shine!

## Creating a Fabulous Portfolio

Here's how to layer your investment portfolio just like you do your wardrobe. It starts with something that keeps you snug, yet can be accessed with ease (don't let your mind wander . . .).

- **The base layer**

  Don't leave home without your good underwear on. Isn't that what your grandmother would say? And make it silk. (Did you know silk has been used as an insulating fabric for centuries and is one of the warmest, yet lightest, fabrics around?)

  The base layer is like an insulator too: your stash of funds for protection against emergencies. You want to invest this money somewhere that is out of reach of your debit card and yet won't cost you any fees if you need to get at the cash quickly. Your goal is to make sure these funds remain intact and accessible, which means choosing an investment vehicle that is low risk (and consequently, relatively low return). High-interest savings accounts or money-market mutual funds are often good choices for base-layer savings.

- **The middle layer**

This is the serviceable, practical layer that you begin with when you start investing in the stock market. Think of these investments like good white cotton shirts and black pencil skirts. You know . . . safe, dependable, wardrobe staples.

Your goal is to hold these companies for a very long time, so look for solid, reliable companies that provide steady returns through interest payments or dividends. Investments to consider for this layer are often major banks, utility companies, government bonds, and low-fee exchange-traded funds (ETFs). A little boring maybe, but very useful. These babies hold up!

- **The top layer**

Growth companies add a little more sex appeal and personality to your portfolio, the way a Chanel tweed blazer (vintage, of course) or a block-print wrap dress can fire up your wardrobe basics.

These companies are not like the workhorses of the middle layer, and they may not provide the lovely reward of regular dividends. However, your goal with these companies is to buy low and watch the company (and the stock price) grow—and subsequently increase the value of your investment. There will likely be ups and downs as these companies react to media stories and strive to meet their growth targets, but if you've done your research and have faith in what they do, you should eventually be rewarded.

- **The accessories layer**

Once you've got your retirement funds and major savings invested, you might find that you have a little extra to invest and you're very attracted to a new start-up company that you've heard could be the next big thing.

Like a bright silk wrap or a pair of chandelier earrings, a small investment in an emerging company has the potential to make a big statement within your portfolio—or it could turn out to be a major faux pas. Your goal with this kind of higher-risk investment is to only use funds you are willing to lose in case the financing for the company doesn't come through or they have distribution problems from which they can't recover. Because there is no known track record for an emerging company, you can do your best to research their industry, their competition, and their financial solvency, but as the fine print always says, "past performance is no guarantee of future results," *especially* when there is a very short past to consider.

---

 **GOLDEN RULE: INVEST IN WHAT YOU KNOW**

As you hand over your debit card (TD) to pay for a pair of Lululemon (LLL) yoga pants, your iPhone (AAPL) rings. So you set down your Starbucks (SBUX) cup and dig through your Coach (COH) bag, to see that your husband texted (T) you from his BlackBerry (RIM). While you're out, he'd like you to pick up socks (HBI) for him at Target (TGT) and stop at the liquor store for some Budweiser (BUD) and Doritos (PEP) because *oh by the way*, he's invited some guys over to watch ESPN (DIS) on the big screen (SNE). You sigh, look down at your daughter, munching on her goldfish crackers (CPB) and think, "What am I, a delivery service now?" So you decide your first stop is the sale at Victoria's Secret (LTD) or maybe even Tiffany & Co. (TIF) to pick yourself up a little something-special on *his* MasterCard (MA). Call it a delivery fee.

You say you don't know what companies to invest in? You know a lot more than you think! Your life is filled with the products of publicly

*(continued)*

---

listed companies. You choose certain brands because you like their style, their taste, or their quality. You know how well their products last and how awesome (or not) their customer service is. You know how popular they are among your friends and which stores are now carrying them (or have dropped them). This is excellent preliminary investment research.

Remember this, you can own Lululemon (the pants), but you can also own Lululemon (the company and stock). Both can literally raise your bottom line.

It's about starting with the companies you know.

## A Little Market 101: What Is an IPO?

A discussion of the stock market is a whole series of books unto itself, but just as we discussed, it helps to get initiated in the basics. After all, your every day—your every *minute*—is affected by the turns of the market and the products that trade therein (just as they are affected by *your* choices—yes, yours!). So let's discuss how an actual stock comes to market.

An initial public offering (IPO) is the means by which a private company "goes public," or begins to offer its shares for sale on a stock exchange.

The process of helping a company "go to market," or prepare its shares for sale, is called "underwriting." When a company decides it would like to sell its shares publicly, it chooses an investment dealer, or a group of them, to act as its underwriter. The underwriter recommends the appropriate type of shares to issue, an initial offering price, and their best estimates on how investors will respond. On behalf of the company, the underwriter files all the appropriate paperwork, such as a preliminary prospectus, with the securities regulators in each province, state, or region where the shares will be sold.

*Real-Life Example*

When Lululemon (with the lower-case *l*, lululemon) decided to go public in July 2007, it turned to Goldman Sachs and Merrill Lynch to underwrite its offering. Do you remember the lineups for the first iPhones that went on sale? Or the frenzy that occurred over new Cabbage Patch dolls back in the 1980s? Same thing here, with that yoga-pant stock creating the equivalent of a half-price designer-shoe sale—can you say market frenzy? The first Lululemon shares offered raised nearly $400 million for the company in *one* day. Hundreds of institutional investors lined up to buy these first shares, a huge sign of early success.

Speaking of which, institutional investors often have the advantage of signing up early for IPOs. (You know how it works, the more you shop at your favourite boutique, the more likely you are to become a preferred customer, getting a sneak preview on new merchandise, access to special sales, and so forth. The same goes in the world of finance. Institutional investors shop a lot.)

The day after their issue, Lululemon shares traded freely on the Toronto and New York stock exchanges, opening at a price of approximately 40 per cent *more* than their IPO price the day before. By the end of the first day on the exchanges, the price went up another 20 per cent or so. Not only did Lululemon successfully raise the capital it needed, early investors had the chance to make a very good immediate profit.

## What Is a "New Issue" and How Is It Different from an IPO?

An IPO represents the first time a private company becomes a publicly listed company. As a public company, its shares are then freely traded on a stock exchange, or secondary market. At some point in the company's evolution, however, a public company may wish to again raise money in the capital markets by offering more shares.

Because these shares will be "new" and originate from the company itself rather than those already trading on the exchange, the process is called a "new issue" or "new offering."

A new issue of shares can be sold to the market in a couple of different ways. The investment dealer, or underwriter, may buy all the shares for their house account, selling them in turn to their clients and the broader market. This is called a "bought deal," because the investment dealer has bought all the shares, ensuring the company will receive the financing it requires.

Alternately, the investment dealer will act as an agent, selling shares on behalf of the company to the broader market without owning the inventory itself. This is called a "best efforts deal."

As with an IPO, institutional investors and large clients often have easiest access to new issues, however individual smaller investors can still participate by being proactive and doing their research. Individual investors often participate in new issues and IPOs without realizing it, through any institutionally managed investments they may hold, such as a pension plan or mutual fund.

For more on the stock market, visit www.GoldenGirlFinance.ca and read "The Fountain of Knowledge—Investing 101" (in the FFAQs section). It's your lowdown on the market, its functions, flaws, and fortitude. As we like to say, drink it up, girlfriend! It's good for you.

## Dividends Are a Girl's Best Friend

Stock prices go up and stock prices go down, but dividends are forever. Do you hear what we are saying?

A return on your investment is really only an idea until you sell your investment. If you buy a stock at $20 and it goes up to $30, you've made a wonderful $10 return on your investment, but you have to sell your stock to actually take that money in. And if it's a good investment, you may not want to sell it for many years.

Dividends are the way a company gives a more immediate reward to its shareholders. The company takes a portion of its annual profits and divvies it up among its shareholders in the form of dividends. This is the company's way of saying: shareholders, we love you.

Investors may choose to receive dividend payments in cash or take part in a dividend reinvestment plan, whereby the dividend money is automatically used to buy more shares in that company. This is the shareholders' way of saying: company, we love you, too.

---

 **DID YOU KNOW? GIMME THE DRIP!**

Companies that issue reliable dividends are typically banks and utilities—boring, conservative, and highly profitable. They also offer a neat trick known to those in the biz as "DRIPS": dividend reinvestment plans. These are an excellent way to grow your savings while averaging out the price you pay for company shares.

For example, imagine you own 100 shares of the Nothing Interesting Colossal Earnings company (NICE). The company pays a quarterly dividend of $0.25 per share. Rather than taking a cheque for $25 every quarter, you enroll in a DRIP. Your $25 will be reinvested, meaning it will be used to buy more shares of NICE. The company's price will fluctuate: some quarters it will be like getting a sale price and your $25 will buy a larger portion of shares; some quarters it will be like a price hike and your $25 won't buy you as much. The dividend payouts may fluctuate as well, depending on how profitable the company was in that quarter. The more shares you own, the more dividends you will receive and the more shares they will buy, which qualifies you for more dividends . . . and so on . . . and so on. Do you get the picture? This is a key tactic in making your money work for you.

## Asset Allocation (a.k.a. Diversification)

Asset allocation is about balancing your portfolio between four main asset classes. This lowers your risk of relying too heavily on any one area of the financial markets. Asset allocation is a bit like having a backup plan; it ensures that your whole nest egg doesn't fall apart if one area of your portfolio fares poorly. (You know, like the nice guy you agreed to marry as a backup plan if you both turned 30 and were still single. My goodness, who knew 30 would feel so *young!*)

### 1. Stocks

Also known as equities. Primarily used for growth and diversification. Depending how much you have to invest, your advisor may recommend company shares, mutual funds (pools of company shares), or exchange-traded funds (also known as ETFs, a hybrid investment that is like a mutual fund in that you invest in a group of companies, but the fund trades on an exchange like a company's shares).

### 2. Bonds

Also known as fixed income. Primarily used to balance the higher-risk investment of equities, by providing conservative and reliable returns.

### 3. Cash

Also known as money markets. This is your high-interest savings account or money-market fund where you stash your savings for emergencies.

### 4. Real estate

For some people, their home represents the biggest portion of their investment portfolio. For others, it is their total investment plan. On the other hand, some people do not own real-estate property, and they can choose to invest in real-estate investment trusts (REITs), which act like a mutual fund in that your investment is pooled with other investors to own large income-producing properties.

### 5. Bonus class

Hedge funds and alternative investments, such as art, vintage cars, and other appreciating assets such as gold (we love *that!*), are often referred to as the fifth asset class. (No matter how much we have tried to tell ourselves otherwise, shoes are not an asset class. Even Louboutins. We know. It's just not fair.)

Hedge funds, in particular, are financial instruments that allow you to hedge against any areas where you might be too heavily invested. For example, if all of your investments are in the technology industry, you might want to invest in a fund that is structured to offset any losses you will suffer if the entire technology industry takes a dive.

It's about mixing things up and keeping the party going . . . even when everyone else has crashed.

## Bonds Have More Fun

Or so they like to think, anyway. In the world of investments, equities are usually the sexier asset class; they come with interesting stories, colourful CEOs, and the promise to send their share prices to the moon! (In reality, they play hot and cold, dropping one day due to some negative publicity, then shooting through the roof on news of a positive deal.)

Bonds, on the other hand, are like the stable, quiet, good guy of the investment world. They do what they say they will, nothing more, nothing less. You know exactly what you are going to get.

A bond is essentially a loan that you are making (not taking, for once). You agree to loan a company or government (the bond issuer) money in exchange for their bond (promise to pay). The issuer guarantees to pay you interest for a specified period of time, then pay back the face value (the principal you loaned them) at a given date in time.

The caveat (there's always a caveat) is that the guarantee is only as reliable as the company or government issuing the bonds. So naturally, those issuers with a shaky reputation will have to cough up a lot more interest to make it appealing for you to invest with them.

Typically, government bonds are considered safer because governments have the recourse of taxpayer dollars if they run into trouble, while companies could go bankrupt. In recent years, however, some governments have been as risky as any company. Portugal, Ireland, Greece, and Spain have all teetered toward the edge of defaulting on their loans.

The bonds with the lowest risk of default pay the lowest interest. Company bonds (or corporate debt) are associated with higher risk than stable governments, so they tend to pay a little more interest. The highest paying and riskiest bonds are those with the highest probability of default and these are known as "high-yield bonds" or "junk bonds." The high interest these bonds pay is great . . . until you find out you're not getting your principal back (big ouch).

The interest rate paid by a bond is also affected by the duration of the bond. If the bond promises to return your principal in a short period of time (say, five years), you are taking less risk than if the bond matures in 30 years. Therefore, the long-term bond will offer you a higher interest rate in order to attract your investment.

Bond markets are huge—about twice the size of equity markets. Most of the investors are large institutions and they receive much better rates than small individual investors. If you want to add bonds to your portfolio, you can buy them individually or you may also consider a low-fee bond mutual fund or a bond ETF. The fund will hold the actual bonds, but the fund itself is not guaranteed and fluctuates with interest rate movements.

**LIFE LESSON: LEARN FROM CARRIE**

"I like my money right where I can see it: in my closet," said Carrie Bradshaw, plucky heroine of *Sex and the City*. Yet even Carrie had to face the financial wall and see the folly of her ways when she realized she had no savings and her attempt to get a loan to buy her apartment was rejected. Carrie had to swallow her pride and go begging to her ex-boyfriend for money. Even that wasn't enough: all her girlfriends had to pony up with some cash as well. Thank goodness it was only television, because in real life, this would be a scenario so mortifyingly and desperately cringe-worthy that it would actually make all those Jimmy Choos and Manolo Blahniks suddenly look *not* so hot.

## Covering Your Assets: How to Manage Risk

Think for a moment about the risks you've taken to get where you are today. As a kid, you probably took a few risks to add to your fun (skipping class), have adventure (learning to skateboard), and try new things (oh no you didn't—you crimped your hair, didn't you!). Though they may seem minor now, these were important lessons in testing your boundaries and learning more about yourself (big hair isn't necessarily better).

As an adult, the risks naturally become bigger: taking a new job, moving to a new city, learning a new language and travelling to foreign countries. When you take risks as an adult, you are still learning about what you are comfortable with, what excites you, and what kind of miracles you can pull off that you never even knew you were capable of (such as landing a one-year work term, in Paris, with less than a month to master fluent French—oh you *did* it, didn't you!).

The fact is that risk is a natural part of your life. You make choices every day that come with the risk of the path not taken and the risk of challenges that earn you sweet rewards of adventure and achievement. You do this by taking calculated risks: weighing the upsides against the downsides, the risks versus the rewards.

When it comes to investments, as in life, there are always risks, just as there are rewards. By avoiding all potential loss, you lose out on the chance for any gain. Let's consider a couple scenarios:

- There is the risk of making an investment, only to watch the market crash and lose some of your hard-earned savings.

- And yet there is also the risk of not putting your money into that investment and missing out on a huge opportunity to greatly increase your wealth.

Depending on how you reacted to each of the above scenarios, you probably know where you stand on the risk-reward pendulum.

For some people, the idea of losing money is enough to keep them up at night; while for others, the thought of missing out on the chance to profit is more than they can bear. Where you fit in the spectrum has a lot to do with your financial goals and your investment horizon. If you're just starting out with the next 40 years to plan for your retirement, your view on investment risk will be much different than if you are in the home stretch with just a couple more years before you retire.

Companies talk a lot about risk management, and some large companies have huge departments dedicated to managing their financial, legal, health-and-safety, and reputational risks. These companies devote great effort to forecasting all the risks that could harm their business and then take proactive steps to minimize those risks.

You can do the same when it comes to your personal situation. Let's take a look at all the risks that might concern you about investing and see how you can handle them in graceful golden-girl style.

- Capital risk

The fear of losing any bit of your capital—what you put into the investment—is the fear that keeps many investors right out of the stock market. Unless there is a guarantee with no potential of default, such as guaranteed investment certificates (GICs) or government savings bonds, then there will be some level of capital risk. Of course, the market knows this, which is why the riskier the investment, the higher the potential return.

✓ **How to manage?** Be a long-term investor. Do your research and once you're sure you've made a good selection, set your strategy and stick with it.

- **Purchasing-power risk**

Those low-risk investments might be very tempting if you're a risk-averse kind of girl. The trouble is, when you tie your money up for a period of time with the expectation of very little return, a little thing called inflation might just bite you in the behind. This means that you hand over your money now (enough, say, to buy a very nice sofa) and then you wait, while inflation makes the prices of everything increase—until the day your money is returned and now all you can afford to buy with it is a very nice throw pillow. You've just lost purchasing power.

✓ **How to manage?** It's all about balance. Stocks and bonds work very nicely together to balance the risk and returns, and hedge against inflation. Like having a salad with your grilled cheese sandwich.

- **Volatility risk**

Markets go up and markets go down; this is a fact of life. Watching your investments go up and down can be stressful. Yet the research shows that over time, equities as a class generally go up. If you've made a plan to hold an investment for a certain amount of time, you have to give it a chance to get there.

✓ **How to manage?** Don't watch the market every day; this is your financial advisor's job. When your sound intellectual framework for decision-making indicates that it's time to review an investment, that's when you look at what is happening and reassess. It's kind of like dieting: you set a goal and stick with your strategy to eat right and exercise more. If you weigh yourself every few hours, you will just get dismayed by all the natural fluctuations and possibly give up too soon.

• **Interest-rate risk**

Those nice, pleasant bonds trade daily and just because you bought it yesterday doesn't mean someone else won't buy it tomorrow at a better rate. The price can change when rates on new issues come out with similar terms and credit ratings. If the new bonds pay more, then the existing bonds lose value; if the new bonds pay less, the existing bonds become more valuable.

✓ **How to manage?** Don't look and don't worry about it. If you hold the bonds to maturity as planned, then any price changes in the interim are irrelevant.

• **Credit risk**

This is the risk that the issuer of the bond you bought doesn't keep up their end of the deal and defaults or goes bankrupt. Less reputable (and therefore riskier) companies or governments pay higher interest rates to compensate for this risk.

✓ **How to manage?** Know to whom you are lending your money. Think of it like lending money to a friend. If the friend is unemployed and has a bad habit of borrowing money and never paying it back, this is a high risk. But if your friend has a great job, is trustworthy, and you know she's good for it, you'll feel a lot safer. When you choose a bond, look for signals of a strong credit reputation. An AAA-rated bond is very unlikely to default.

- **Company or industry risk**

  You know what happens when you put all your eggs in one basket, don't you? If all your investments are in real estate and the whole sector crashes, then your house price will also suffer a blow. Similarly, a stock's price reflects the market's expectations for that company and its industry. If the whole industry is hurt by a new development, all the companies in that industry are at risk of losing value.

  ✓ How to manage? Diversify, diversify, diversify! Spread your investments across companies within a sector (mutual funds and ETFs are very useful for this), and balance your portfolio by investing in a variety of sectors.

- **Geographical risk**

  Typically investors prefer to invest in companies in their own country, whether out of patriotism or familiarity. Yet if all your investments are located in the same country or geographical region and the area suffers an earthquake, a hurricane, or a political crisis (everything from a change in government policy to an all-out military coup), your investment portfolio will take a hit.

  ✓ **How to manage?** Choose companies or funds that invest in different regions around the world. Even without a catastrophe, you will have better access to more of the world's great companies and great investment opportunities if you stretch your horizons.

**LIFE LESSON: INVEST BEYOND YOUR BORDERS**

Investing in your country's resources makes absolute sense. You have to give back to your own. But don't let that stop you from exploring all that the investment *world* (quite literally) has to offer.

Take Canada, for example. Thanks to its strong market of resources, commodities, and financial stocks, it has fared well in recent economic downturns; but looking at it globally, Canada accounts for only about 3 per cent of the world's stock-market capitalization, and many top global companies are available only through foreign markets. So if you limit your holdings to Canadian companies, you're effectively cutting yourself off from 97 per cent of the world's investment opportunities (think pharmaceuticals, health care, and other interesting prospects beyond the borders of the Great White North). A smart investor knows to think local *and* global.

## The Team that Takes Care of You

When you are sick, you visit a doctor. When you sign a pre-nup, you visit a lawyer. When you want to buy a house, you call a real-estate agent. And when you cave in between appointments and buy that home-colour highlighting kit (and turn your "blonde" hair orange), you haul those damaged tresses to your hairstylist ASAP!

They're called professionals, and they help you to navigate complicated (and common-place) situations or areas where you lack expertise. So when you want to invest your hard-earned money, why on earth wouldn't you call an investment professional for help?

These days, investment professionals come in many different varieties and are licensed within their markets to work with different aspects of your finances (investments, insurance, banking, and taxes). Typically, an investment advisor (or stockbroker) can help you with your securities portfolio, including stocks, bonds, mutual funds, and ETFs.

A financial planner, as another example, might not be licensed to trade stocks for you, but can give you broader guidance on your overall financial picture, including budgeting, saving, insurance, taxes, and estate planning.

The most important factor is to recognize that your financial advisor is an essential member of the team that takes care of you. Like your lawyer, your housekeeper, your hair stylist, and that very cute barista who makes your latte just the way you like it, these are the people with whom you surround yourself to get things done.

To bring us back to Chapter 1, you are the chairperson of your own personal board of directors. You set the targets (no-foam latte; long layers at the back; 10 per cent annual return) and the experts you've assembled around you help you to achieve those goals.

Choose your professional posse wisely.

---

**WHEN CONTROL ISN'T COOL: IT'S *YOUR* MONEY, HONEY**

Your money is, well, your money. Part of the reason why it is important to develop your own network of experts is to maintain your independence and ensure that the financial decisions that you make are in your own best interest (repeat, *your own best interest!*).

If you find yourself in situations where others are trying to influence the decisions you make about your money (perhaps, to their own best advantage), lean on your team of advisors for help. Let them be your compass to ensure that your actions are consistent with your financial plan. Remember, it is *your* money.

---

## Ways to Find a Financial Advisor

So you need an advisor? Here are some ways of going about finding a good one:

- **Word of mouth:** Ask a friend or another advisor such as your accountant, lawyer, banker, or even your dentist who they would recommend. (Hey, they make a lot of money, so they're probably pretty picky about with whom they invest their loot).

- **Go to a seminar or course:** The advisor who is hosting will likely contact you afterward, and while this may feel a little awkward, look at the seminar and the follow-up as a chance to hear what they have to say, assess a fit, and learn something (probably score a pretty nice lunch or dinner, too).

- **Research specific firms:** Ask the branch manager to recommend someone whose practice is suitable for someone in your position.

- **Ask your personal banker:** Chances are, if you're already doing your day-to-day banking with your chosen bank, you've built a relationship of trust. The result? They should know and understand your current situation. This is a great opportunity to discuss your needs and be referred to a professional within their system who can best serve your profile, requirements, and goals.

## Choosing the Right Advisor

Like any professional with whom you work, you want to find someone that fits; someone who you feel comfortable with, even if you need to ask, shall we say, *novice* questions (hey, no such thing!); someone who, above all, you can trust. When you find an advisor who you think has potential, it's time to give him or her an interview. Here's how:

- **Ask for a no-obligation consultation,** a chance to get a feel for each other.

  ✓ Does he or she use confusing jargon?

  ✓ Do you feel uncomfortable sharing your financial information with him or her?

✓ Do you get the impression that he or she is more concerned with his or her own retirement plan than yours?

- **Ask about his or her target client,** the type of investor with whom he or she has experience or prefers.

  ✓ Are you a fit?

  ✓ Is your account too small? (You may not get the service you want.)

  ✓ Is your account too large or your financial situation too complex? (The advisor may not be experienced enough to counsel you in the issues you face, such as trusts, estates, or corporate entities.)

- **Ask about the process of working together.**

  ✓ Will there be regularly scheduled reviews or will you talk on an as-needed basis?

  ✓ Does he or she offer a full range of financial planning, to cover all the services you need?

  ✓ Will he or she work with you to create an investment policy statement (the official term for your "sound intellectual framework") that defines what you will be investing in, as well as measures your appetite and expectations for risk and return?

- **After your initial meeting, follow up with some homework.**

  ✓ Obtain references from the advisor's existing clients and call them to see if they are satisfied with the level of service they've received.

  ✓ Next, check the advisor's credentials. Are they registered with the provincial or state securities commission where you reside?

  ✓ Find out if there have been complaints filed against him or her with the securities commission and what were the results. (This information is typically available on-line.)

---

 **GOLDEN RULE: MORE FROM MR. BUFFETT**

"Beware of geeks bearing formulas."—Warren Buffett.[6]

A good advisor will help you to understand your financial situation and your opportunities for investing, not create more confusion. If you leave your advisor's office thoroughly bewildered by ratios and charts, and his or her answers to your questions only create more mystery, perhaps it's time to find a new advisor or at the very least, get a second opinion!

You don't need to be her best friend or want to introduce him to your single girlfriend, but you do need to feel a rapport, a comfort level, and a meeting of minds to plow through the thick and thin of the investment world.

---

## Paying for the Service

Investment professionals can work with you in a number of ways. These are people who are used to dealing with money all day long, so do not be shy about asking how their fees work. And keep asking questions until you fully understand!

Here are some common ways fees are passed on to the client:

- **Fee for advice only**

  These professionals will charge you for their time (similar to a lawyer), to help you put together a plan (your sound intellectual

---

[6]Charlie Rose, "An Exclusive Conversation with Warren Buffett," 1 October 2008, http://www.charlierose.com/view/interview/9284

framework) and make recommendations on how to structure your overall financial situation so you will be able to reach your goals. They provide a service, but not the execution of buying or selling of any investments.

- **Fee based on assets**

  These professionals will charge you an annual fee calculated as a percentage of the assets you have invested with them. These individuals will help establish a plan for your investments, while also executing the buying and selling of investments on your behalf.

- **Commission based**

  This type of arrangement is increasingly less common. The investment professional will not charge you an annual fee, but instead charge you a fee for any activity that occurs in your account, such as buying and selling transaction costs on stocks or bonds. This may also include imbedded fees on mutual funds (they are not free) or new issues.

- **Blended pricing**

  Some advisors will charge you a fee for the advice component of their work for you, as well as commissions for trading activity.

## The Takeaway

Which fee schedule is right for you? There are no right or wrong answers here. The important thing is to monitor what those fees amount to on a monthly, yearly, and periodic basis, and determine if the level of service and performance is worth the financial output.

**DID YOU KNOW? FEES ARE NEGOTIABLE**

With respect to paying fees to your investment advisors, it's important to understand what you are paying for and how that is structured. Fees themselves are quite often negotiable, and depending on how you pay, may become tax deductible.

Structuring your fees in a way that allows you to pay them efficiently (making them tax deductible when possible)—and paying *less* (if possible)—should not be ignored. Anything you pay in fees effectively reduces your overall return, therefore it's important to have an open and honest discussion with your advisor to understand exactly how you are paying for the services they are providing.

Consider this: overpaying on fees and/or not ensuring tax efficiency with your fees can add up over time. For example, a 1 per cent fee difference on a $300,000 portfolio growing at an average of 8 per cent over 10 years is $54,000 (now, that's a lot of vacations, a brand-new kitchen, or a really great college education). So don't be shy: this is an important discussion to have with your advisor. It doesn't always mean that the fees presented will be reduced, but it does put the advisor on alert that you're fee savvy.

## What about Discount or On-line Brokerages?

The great thing about stock markets is that they are accessible. You don't actually need a full-service financial advisor to participate; rather, you can do it yourself on-line. If you have the interest and ability to do your own research and follow the markets, then on-line investing can be a smart and economical way to go.

One caveat: beginner investors would be wise to start out by working with a professional to learn how to make trades, buy mutual funds, and read the stock tables. As you become acquainted with the language and begin to see the way the markets are affected by current events, you will grow in your confidence and experience.

Investing requires knowledge, discipline, and the ability to keep your head when all those around are losing theirs. Like any other area of your life—from your accountant to your plumber—if the service of a professional is valuable to you, then it might be worth paying a fee to let someone else take care of the details. Do a little dabbling, but perhaps leave the big picture up to those who don't squeeze in their transactions between work meetings, grocery shopping, and car pooling (or whatever else it is you do with your limited time!).

## Working with a Financial Advisor: the Six Essential Steps

In any area of life, success is often dictated by your ability to set goals and articulate those goals. Better yet, to write down a plan to achieve those goals. This is especially true when it comes to money. Unfortunately, you can't just hand over your pile of beans to your financial advisor and rely on her to magically create a beanstalk. You're in this together and the first step is to make sure you understand one another and your goals.

Once you've chosen an investment professional to work with, there are six main steps you can expect to go through in the process of working together.

### 1. The discovery process

This is not so different than when you meet Mr. Right and you stay up all night talking and wanting to learn everything about each other. Essentially, what you are doing is a discovery. If he's interested in you, he wants to know where you came from, how you spend your time, and what your dreams and plans are for the future.

Similarly, a good advisor will take great care to gather as much information as possible, so she can understand your needs and those of your family. She will want to understand the motivations behind your long-term financial goals, your income requirements, your tax situation, and your estate matters. This meeting is critical for both you and your advisor, as she will use this information to start developing your plan and for your account documentation as well.

Take the time to review these documents carefully when they are presented to you for signature as they will be used for the protection of both you and your advisor in the event of a dispute.

## 2. The snapshot

Your advisor will want to get a picture of where you are today in terms of your goals. She will want to know what you've got (assets) and what you owe (liabilities). She will ask you about your financial priorities and limitations, as well as any risks or opportunities that you might be facing financially.

## 3. Developing your strategy

Here it is, the moment you've been waiting for! Together, you will create your sound intellectual framework for making decisions. Based on the information she has gathered through the discovery process and your current snapshot, she will recommend an action plan that includes an asset mix strategy, target investment recommendations, and any insurance, tax, or estate-planning implications. She will review this with you carefully, so you understand the steps that will follow and how you will proceed with buying and selling any of the securities in the plan.

## 4. The execution of your plan

Once you have approved the strategy and are comfortable that it meets your criteria for making decisions, as well as aligns with your goals, it's time to put these plans into action.

Just a reminder to make sure that you are clear on any fees or transaction costs associated with the execution of the plan.

### 5. Measuring your progress

Now that your plan is in action, you will want to meet regularly with your advisor to review the progress of your portfolio. Perhaps it's quarterly or semi-annually. If you prefer to have regular phone calls with your advisor, make sure she is highly accessible to you and proactive in letting you know if she recommends changes to the plan along the way.

### 6. The maintenance

Your hair requires regular touch-ups, so why wouldn't your investments? Life always brings changes and issues, such as marriage, divorce, children, job loss, or inheritance, that can radically alter your goals, your outlook, and your cash flow.

Always remember to keep your advisor informed so that you can adjust your financial plan or strategy accordingly; this is one of *your* most important roles in the process. Your ongoing input is key. You're in this together, babe!

---

 **DID YOU KNOW? DEBT-AND-CASH-FLOW PLANS**

Your financial advisor is not just there to help you with your investments. A debt-and-cash-flow plan is often a first step before determining how much you have to invest. This kind of plan will address how you will pay down your debts, as well as how to manage day-to-day spending and major purchases.

You will need to bring a lot of homework to the table, including summaries of your debts and an outline of your current expenses. Your

*(continued)*

advisor may have recommendations on how to structure your debt, as well as spending advice. For many people, financial planning to get their cash flow under control is essential to helping them get on a sound financial track for the future.

## What to Do When Things Don't Feel Right

There may come a time when you're just not sure if you're getting the right advice. Or you don't know why exactly, but you have a feeling that you're paying more than necessary for a certain service.

The first step is to address the situation directly. Talk to your advisor, and if necessary, his or her supervising manager. Trust your instincts and never be shy about asking the tough questions.

If you are concerned that there might be something seriously amiss with your account, ask to speak with the firm's compliance manager who is responsible for ensuring the firm follows legal and other regulations. A large firm may also employ an ombudsman, someone whose job it is to investigate client problems and complaints.

You may also choose to get independent advice from someone who is more knowledgeable in financial matters than you are; lawyers, seasoned investors, and money managers can be good choices. Don't let your instincts be swept aside. If something doesn't feel right, there is probably reason to be concerned, or at least, investigate further.

Make sure you have all your records organized and make notes of any communications and meetings that you have with your advisors. In a situation of "he said-she said" (or whatever parties were involved), you need to be prepared to back up your position and stand your ground.

We know your life is busy and when you have experts helping you, there is a big temptation to leave all the details up to them; however, the best way to avoid mismanagement of your affairs is to bite the bullet and pay attention. Keep thorough records and read all the reports and notices issued by your advisors. If you don't understand something, ask for clarification.

The vast majority of professional advisors do act in their clients' best interests, but it's up to you to make sure your interests are clearly expressed to your advisor. After all, no one cares more about your money than you do.

## You've Got Game

And there you have it! Feeling any wiser, calmer, pumped, or prepared about your investing future? This isn't about making you an expert, but encouraging you to get engaged, get connected, and surround yourself with experts of all the right kinds.

Suit up, girlfriend. It's time you got in the game. Planning for your retirement comes next.

# 8

## The Best Third of Your Life

### *Finance and Retirement*

### Living Long and Living Well

There once was a time, not so long ago, when retirement was surely wasted on the old. Given a gold watch and packed off with a pension, people could expect to spend 5 to 15 years in retirement, mainly playing cards, adjusting their dentures, and waiting for infrequent visits from their grandchildren.

These days, 60 is the new 40. Over the past couple of generations, retirement has undergone a welcome makeover. Travel the world, pursue your favourite sports, take up a new career (or a new certain someone), all the while looking as hot as Helen Mirren (rocking a red bikini in Puglia, now *that's* inspiration!).

Healthier lifestyles and medical advances mean that we are all living longer (and women longer than men), and many of us are striving to retire at a younger age than our parents or grandparents. Indeed, these days, you can expect your retirement to last 30 years or more. If you retire at 60, there's a good chance you could live to age 90, making retirement a third of your life!

It boils down to this: you've got a whole lot of living—and spending—left to do! So how to live long and live *well* . . .

## The Drama of Retirement

In theatre and screenwriting circles, much homage is paid to Aristotle's classic three-act structure. Aristotle was a clever guy; it's no accident that the three acts roughly parallel the way we live our lives.

Traditionally, the first act introduces the heroine and sets up her situation, much like finding yourself by the age of 30. The second act sees the main character pursuing her goals, such as mid-life career climb, marriage, and raising children, while conflicts and obstacles threaten to undermine her success (oh, you've had a few!). The third act (hello, Miss Sixty!) brings resolution: our heroine overcomes her obstacles to achieve her goals and lives happily ever after. (Or, in the case of tragedies, she does *not* meet her goals, suffers terribly, and the world at large learns a valuable lesson.) Hmmm . . . which would you prefer?

Whether your third act is a comedy, drama, or tragedy is totally up to you. It comes down to this: in retirement, there is not much that can't be improved with a healthy savings plan on which you can rely.

And rely, you must. Despite all those ads for Florida vacation rentals and bank mutual funds depicting lovely white-haired couples walking hand in hand into the sunset, research tells us that "retirement is very often lived alone, whether by choice, or as the result of divorce or the death of a spouse."[1] (We like to quote Jane Austen from her 1815 novel *Emma*, "a single woman, of good fortune, is always respectable".)

Knowing you have enough savings and income to keep you well funded throughout your retirement alleviates day-to-day stress

---

[1] BMO Retirement Institute, "Divergent Paths to Retirement: How Men and Women Plan Differently," BMO Financial Group, April 2011, http://www.bmo.com/pdf/mf/prospectus/en/11-558_Retirement_Report_April_E.pdf

and allows you to make choices that will feed your soul and make you happy.

Of course, your golden nest egg will need time to grow; hence, the reason financial advisors are so adamant about getting you to start saving early, thus benefiting from the magic of compound interest. As our friend Warren Buffett once said, "Someone's sitting in the shade today because someone planted a tree a long time ago."[2]

Well, we want to see *you* lounging under that shady tree (protecting your age-defying beauty from the sun's harmful rays, of course), so let's get planting!

## Be the Tree: A New-Age Moment

Before we begin to discuss savings and income, it's worth spending a little more time on that shady tree. Many people get hung up on retirement's big brass ring without really grasping what it will mean for them day to day. Retirement in theory sounds blissful; retirement in practice can be a shock.

Now close your eyes (come on, work with us!). Imagine you have been retired for a full year, and you are sitting under a shady tree, feeling utter contentment. Consider:

- ✓ What kind of tree are you sitting under? A palm tree on a beach in the Caribbean? A Douglas fir at your cottage? The maple tree in your backyard? A scotch pine on a snowy ski hill?
- ✓ Imagine the sounds you hear: children laughing, music playing, or pristine silence?
- ✓ Are you sweating from a workout or wrapped in a cozy blanket?
- ✓ What do you smell? Sea air or steaming coffee?
- ✓ Are you alone or is someone sitting with you?

---

[2] James O'Loughlin, *The Real Warren Buffett: Managing Capital, Leading People* (Boston, MA: Nicholas Brealey, 2004).

✓ What were you doing *before* you sat down under the tree?

✓ What activities are waiting for you once you stand up?

✓ What are you wearing?

✓ How do you feel? Energized, relaxed, focused?

Use all of your senses to imagine your tree scene with as much detail as you can. Write down everything you've imagined. If you do the exercise again in a few months or a few years, compare notes to see how the circumstances of your image change.

Now, we don't mean to get all New Agey on you, but there is some reasoning and truth behind this exercise. The images that you visualize in your tree scene can give you important clues with respect to your needs and desires for your post-work lifestyle. Think:

✓ How will you spend your time?

✓ What routines and activities will keep you busy?

✓ What plans or projects will you tackle?

✓ How will your quality of life change: for the worse *and* for the better?

Because you see, *where* you choose to retire and *what* you plan to do when you get there will drastically change the way you structure your finances and your retirement plan.

## Getting Started: Age-Appropriate Tips

Women are legendary planners. We like to plan. You may even have found yourself at some point making a plan to plan ("Let's meet for lunch and plan our vacation!"). This is an excellent trait—do not let anyone (*ahem*—husband, boyfriend, brother) tell you otherwise. When it comes to your retirement, you can never plan too far ahead or start saving too early.

Your age and your distance from the "big R" will naturally affect how aggressive your plans and tactics are in terms of savings and strategy. Consider these age-appropriate tips:

- **In your 20s and 30s**

  When retirement is 20 or 30 years away, you can (and should) be stashing away funds, even though you may not have a clue yet how you intend to spend those golden years. (Heck, you may not even know how you want to spend this weekend!) It won't always be easy, but you have two very valuable things going for you at this point:

  1. **Compound interest,** which can exponentially increase any drop-in-the-bucket funds you add.

  2. **A long investment horizon,** which means you have the opportunity to invest in equities that may be on the higher end of the risk scale, but do have the potential for higher returns.

Your goal at this point of your life is to slowly but surely build wealth. Plant those seeds now!

- **In your 40s**

  You may be facing some of your biggest savings challenges during these years. Between mortgages, cottages, and sending kids to school and university, your retirement savings can easily take a back seat. Yet these are the critical years when you must get serious about your retirement savings. This is your chance to make up for any lost time and replenish any savings you may have raided.

  At this point, your vision of how you want to spend your retirement may be starting to take shape. You have a better idea of the lifestyle you will expect and the income that will be required to fund it. You may even have that villa under the

Tuscan sun already picked out. This is good. It's much easier to save for something when you have an actual target in sight.

Your goal is to ensure that despite your other financial obligations, you are regularly contributing to your retirement funds. You still have 20 some years to go, so you can maintain an aggressive yet well-balanced investment portfolio.

· **In your 50s**

It's go time. You can see yourself on the deck chair already. You can almost taste the Brunello di Montalcino you plan to sip (during a little sojourn in Italy perhaps?). Whether you've decided to spend your retirement pursuing a dream second career or taking a permanent vacation, this is the point when you must meet with your financial advisor to make sure you are on track with your savings and to figure out a plan B if you're not as far ahead as you would like.

While a basic rule of thumb is to plan to have access to 70 per cent of your pre-retirement income upon retirement, an advisor can help you to determine a more specific retirement income level based on your actual expenses and projections of those expenses. Your goals now are to:

1. **Aggressively ramp up** the amount you're putting into savings.

2. **Shift your investment strategy** to a lower-risk wealth preservation mode.

3. **Eliminate your debt** (yes this includes your mortgage, if you can). Living on a fixed income is a whole lot easier without looming debt payments.

· **In your 60s**

Yippee! If you haven't already stepped over the threshold into retirement, you are likely poised to do so soon. We don't mean to rain on your parade, but managing your expenses, paying down debt, and even contributing to your savings are still concerns, perhaps now more than ever. You've got a good 30 years ahead of you (or more!), and despite your new seniors' discount card, the cost of health care, gas, food, and everything else is still rising. Your goals are to:

1. **Make your money last.**

2. **Make your third act the best time of your life!**

 **HINDSIGHT**

*As an advisor, I've worked with many clients as they cross the threshold into retirement. Despite aggressively saving for many years (decades!) to reach that point, very few people stop and think about how they will feel about going from earning a paycheque every two weeks and an annual bonus to living off savings and government benefits.*

*Making the psychological shift to live off (and therefore spend) your hard-earned savings requires a huge change in mindset. Many new retirees have a difficult time with the idea of living off investment income or depleting their investment capital. Fear sets in—and sometimes panic—wondering whether it will be enough. How can it possibly be enough?*

*Just as a pre-retirement client requires a plan for accumulating her savings, a plan for managing your retirement income is equally critical. This will give you a blueprint to see and understand all of the sources of income you will have access to and guidance for how best to draw upon these sources over time, in order to generate the highest after-tax income possible.*

*It's amazing how many people overlook this step and wander into their retirement years quite blindly. Bottom line: if your financial advisor has not suggested helping you design a retirement income plan, make sure you request one.*

## Turbocharge Your Registered Retirement Plan

With their potent combination of tax deductions and tax-deferred compound growth, registered plans are the financial equivalent of an anti-aging wrinkle cream: essential for women of a "certain age." Here are a few ways that smart women get more out of their registered savings plans:

- **Do it now, do it often**

  Amateurs contribute to their savings plans annually. You, savvy investor, will make monthly or biweekly contributions, right out of your paycheque. This will create more opportunity for compound interest to do its magic multiple thing.

- **Max it out**

  Governments provide annual limits as to how much you can put into a registered plan and they typically increase each year. If you add just $30 extra each week (a night out at the movies!), this will add up to more than $1,500 a year.

- **The virtuous refund cycle**

  Contributions to registered plans are tax deductible, so if you contribute as much as you can, there's a good chance you will receive a tax refund. Take that refund and put it into your registered plan and, thereby, earn yourself another refund . . . and a nicely growing nest egg. Consider that an extra $500 invested every year for 30 years, earning 6 per cent annually, will add up to $41,900 to your retirement fund. Nice saving, lady!

- **Go for growth**

  When you have a long investment horizon, growth stocks give you a better chance at a bigger return. There is typically more risk of volatility with growth stocks, but the advantage of staying invested longer means that those bumps tend to even out in the long term.

**GOLDEN RULE: A WORD ON THE COST OF LIVING**

No matter where you live, health care and housing costs are likely to go up. Government revenues can't seem to keep up with health-care budgets, particularly as the aging baby boomer demographic moves through the system. Don't expect any cost breaks for either your health or your home. Calculate a cost of living increase into your retirement income plan.

## Retirement Reality Checks

- **"My kids are my retirement plan."**

  We've actually heard of people who rationalize having three or more kids (and the expenses that come with it) by assuming that at least one offspring will be über-successful (and therefore make up for the lack of saving Mom and Dad did in raising the giant brood). Hello! Very bad idea!

  Your kids (like your man) should never be your retirement plan, even if you are convinced little Jack is going to be a hockey star or little Ella will be a brain surgeon. Furthermore, you simply can't afford to sacrifice your own retirement money for the sake of funding everything for your children, particularly your adult children.

  If you can't afford to pay for their full college tuition while also contributing to your retirement savings, pay yourself first and then help your kids find ways to supplement their school costs through scholarships, loans, and summer jobs. They will appreciate this later when taking you out for lunch in your old age is not a burden . . . it's a *pleasure*.

- **"My husband is my retirement plan."**

  Unfortunately, your loving hubby won't be around forever. Statistically speaking, there's a good chance you will outlive him.

Are you sufficiently protected financially? Adequate life insurance can help defray any debts and taxes on his estate, but you must also ensure that any assets will be smoothly transferred to you in order to reduce those nasty taxes. Your husband's pension plan will also likely provide for a beneficiary entitlement, though take heed: the extra income from that will fall solely on your tax shoulders.

- **"My house is my retirement plan."**

For the past few decades, many people have invested heavily in real estate, expecting that the markets and their home values would rise forever. When it comes time to retire, they would sell their home, downsize to more modest digs, and live off the difference. If you are one of these people, with all your retirement eggs in the home basket, we'd like to give you a few points to ponder, just to make sure you are prepared:

- **Beware of being at the mercy of the markets**

   As we saw in 2008 and 2009, real-estate markets are not immune to falling. There is no guarantee that when you are ready to sell your house, the market will be on an upswing.

- **Watch your weight(ings)**

   If, in addition to your primary home, you are invested in other properties, such as vacation homes, commercial property, or shares in a real-estate investment trust, you may be even more vulnerable to market swings and it would be wise to balance your portfolio with other asset classes.

- **Believe in equities**

   Investors often think of real estate as safe, dependable, and always increasing in value. Yet, historical data has proven that over the long term, the stock market has provided better average annual compound returns than any other asset class, including real estate.

- **Selling takes time**

  Real estate is not a liquid investment. Even if you want to sell your home fast and need the funds in a hurry, real estate will take its sweet time. You will need to prepare the property for sale, list it, and wait for closing.

- **Selling costs money**

  Just as there is no quick way to get out of real estate, there is no cheap way either. Agent commissions, legal fees, land-transfer taxes, and moving costs will all eat into your sale profits, not to mention the cost of doing any upgrades prior to listing for sale.

- **Sideways sizing**

  Quite often, people intend to downsize their home in order to save costs, yet end up buying a smaller, but swankier condo with high strata fees that offset any savings from home maintenance or gardening. Do the math to ensure that you are downsizing your costs (and not merely your square footage!).

---

 **DID YOU KNOW? PUT IT IN REVERSE!**

As you approach retirement, you will likely become acquainted with the term *reverse mortgage*. This option is highly appealing for many retirees looking for a way to increase their cash flow by using the

*(continued)*

equity that is stored in their home, without actually selling the house. How does this work?

- A reverse mortgage is a loan against your home that you don't have to pay back until you sell the house.

- The loan will be based on the value of your home.

- There are no monthly payments. Interest on the loan will be added to the principal you owe.

- You can use the loan as cash flow or to finance the purchase of other real estate, such as a vacation property.

- Lending rates and fees may be higher than other mortgages or regular loans.

- By using the equity in your home now, you will deplete the value when it is one day sold—something to think about for your estate plan.

## Show Me the Money: Where Do I Get My Retirement Income?

One fine day, you will wake up, yawn, stretch your arms, smile to the world, and announce, "Today, I am retired!" Awesome. Then what? Where will the money come from to pay for your golfing lessons and your Diane Von Furstenberg beach kaftans?

If you're like most people, your retirement income will be gleaned from a variety of sources: government pensions, company pensions, and your own savings. Let's consider these sources:

- **Government pensions**

  If you have worked full-time, you and your employer paid premiums into a government pension plan (deducted from your paycheques). Upon application, you will receive payments representing a fraction of what you paid into the system. Many governments also provide modest age-based pensions and other top-up benefits that are calculated based on your overall income.

- **Company pensions**

   While you were working, you likely paid into a company pension plan, also through premiums on your paycheque. If you have a defined benefit pension plan, the calculation of your payments will depend on how many years you worked for the company and your salary. If you have a defined contribution pension plan, your income will be based on the performance of the funds you and your employer paid into the plan.

- **Registered retirement savings**

   Known in the United States as 401Ks and in Canada as RRSPs, these are personal savings accounts that provide tax sheltering for the purposes of saving for one's own retirement. Within a registered plan, you may hold a variety of financial investments such as stocks, bonds, GICs, mutual funds, ETFs, and other securities.

- **Non-registered savings**

   These correspond to any other savings or investment accounts you have that are *not* registered with the government as tax-efficient retirement savings vehicles. Many people choose to hold investments that are inherently tax efficient (for example, dividend-generating funds) outside of a registered plan, while using their registered plan for investments that would otherwise trigger capital gains and other investment income taxes.

## Save Money, Reduce Taxes

In Canada, it is wise to consider maxing out your yearly tax-free savings account (TFSA), approximately $5,000 per year, indexed to inflation.

In a regular non-registered account, typically every dollar of investment income (i.e., interest, dividends) is taxed, as are your capital gains. What this basically means is that you have to earn more than a dollar to get a dollar (how much more will depend on your tax bracket).

In an RRSP, you get a tax break up front, but once you start withdrawals . . . oops! Then comes the taxing part, literally. With the TFSA, on the other hand, you don't pay tax on the growth of your investments. As in, you make a dollar and you get to keep that *whole* dollar.

Better still, you don't just have to let your money sit there. This is about much more than the *savings* in the name would suggest; rather, think about its earnings (a.k.a., growth) potential, including the possibility of investing your TFSA funds in:

- mutual funds;
- money-market funds;
- cash deposits;
- GICs;
- publicly traded securities; or
- government and corporate bonds.

Indeed, it pays to talk to your advisor or bank representative about opening a TFSA and seeing how you can take advantage of this very appealing investment vehicle for your savings needs. Tax-free—we *love* the sound of that!

---

 **LIFE LESSON: SWINGING SINGLE IN RETIREMENT**

Without the ability to income split, being single can be costly. Plan carefully, since any retirement income you receive will need to be

*(continued)*

reported solely on your own tax return, rather than split with a spouse. If you hit a certain income ceiling, you may lose eligibility for some government benefits and end up paying higher taxes to boot.

Widows who receive their spouses' registered funds don't pay taxes on the transfer, but are fully responsible for paying the taxes on any income that follows. Your portion of your spouse's pension plan benefits will also raise your income and trigger more taxes. From a financial perspective, the death of a husband doesn't cut the expenses in half; however, when there is only one person to claim the income, the effect can be close to cutting that *income* in half.

Single retirees sometimes choose to share accommodations in order to live comfortably in a larger property or in an area that suits their lifestyle (hello Blanche, Sophia, Rose, and Dorothy!). If you do buy a house with someone, make sure you have a legal agreement in place that addresses ownership transfer if one person dies, remarries, or for whatever reason wants out of the arrangement.

## What If I Don't Have Enough to Retire?

You've scrimped and saved. You've met with your financial advisor. You've done all the calculations. No matter which way you look at it, the ends are refusing to meet. Your plan to spend your golden years yachting around the Mediterranean is looking more like a canoe trip on the Great Lakes (bathtub paddling, anyone?). What do you do?

The way we see it, you've got five options to offset a shortfall in your income projection:

### 1. Delay retirement

One choice is to retire later, or phase into retirement by working part-time or taking a self-employed or contract position, perhaps with your former employer.

## 2. Downsize

Reduce your expenses and consider downsizing your home. Before undertaking this, however, do the math on the cost of staying versus all of the costs that come with selling, buying, and moving.

## 3. Reverse mortgage

Consider using a reverse mortgage to increase your retirement cash flow.

## 4. Change your expectations

You may find that there are some things on your wish list that you are willing to give up in order to be able to live comfortably and without stress.

## 5. Super save

Depending on your time frame, you can increase your nest egg by saving more or increasing investment risk to boost returns. Both of these tactics require the benefit of time to be successful, so the closer you are to retirement, the less feasible they will be.

---

### WHEN CONTROL ISN'T COOL: ELDER ABUSE

Women, who typically live longer and end up alone, can be particularly vulnerable to elder abuse, particularly when it comes to their finances. Sadly, this type of behaviour may come from family members, who may be facing their own financial challenges, or for whatever reason, feel that they are entitled to exert this type of power.

If you or a family member is being subjected to financial abuse, seek assistance to resolve the situation *immediately*. Part of the benefit

(*continued*)

of having your own network of advisors is the access to assistance and support in times of trouble. Seek assistance from your lawyer, investment advisor, or other key advisors to resolve the matter, and don't hesitate to contact the authorities if you believe a crime has been committed.

Above all else, take care of yourself. These situations can understandably be traumatic, so put aside the embarrassment and guilt you might feel (this is *not* your fault) and lean on those who love you. They (and you) will be glad you did.

## Workin' It: Post-Retirement Careers

The thing about work is that when you *have* to get up in the morning and go to your job, it feels suspiciously like . . . work. Once you are retired, however, and freed from the shackles of daily employment, you might hear yourself offering to "help out" at the designer-clothing boutique where you usually shop. Or you might look at your beautiful, rambling old home and think, "I could turn this into a B&B!" You get the picture.

You may be surprised at how much you miss your former colleagues and the sense of purpose you gained from your career. You may find yourself lunching with former colleagues, staying on top of industry news, and offering to advise friends with their projects and business plans.

Retirement can have the effect of renewing your passion for work, whether it's the same kind of work you've built your career on or exploring a field that is completely new to you. When it's no longer a chore, you start to look upon your professional capabilities and the possibilities of work in a whole new way.

We know of women who spent their whole lives working to make ends meet and save for retirement, only to find that the hobby or passion they pursued during their retirement led to starting a business and earning even more money than they did before retirement.

Think of it this way: the first stage of your retirement can act as a sabbatical. You know, time to reflect on the work you've done, your achievements, and what your logical (or completely illogical) next steps might be. And once you've had a chance to reflect, just do it!

---

 **GOLDEN RULE: EXTRA INCOME**

Be aware that any extra income you earn will affect your ability to collect certain government-sponsored retirement benefits. You will have to review your tax situation and your registered plan details. In addition, when returning to work, consider how you wish to be employed, as an employee or as an independent contractor—and the tax advantages and disadvantages of each. In short, speak to your financial advisor about the implications of pursuing a new career; he or she can help you to structure your finances to your best advantage.

---

## Your Legacy and Your Estate

While you're kicking back under that shady tree, enjoying your glorious retirement, we just want to remind you of a few affairs you need to have in order during your third act of life.

Getting your estate in order is like cleaning out your closets. You avoid doing it as long as possible, but once you dedicate the time and just get it done, you feel a thousand times better (and wonder why it took you so long to get it organized in the first place)!

The purpose of an estate plan is to provide financial security for your family. It also creates a legacy for you to leave behind, ensuring that your wishes and directions are carried out when it comes to the distribution of your assets and the care of your loved ones.

Here are the important areas to cover when updating your estate plan:

- **Your will**

  This is your opportunity to be clear about your intentions when you die. If you aren't, you may create disharmony among your surviving family members, as well as leave the process in the time-consuming hands of the courts to determine.

  Assets may be transferred between spouses without tax consequences, but when the second spouse dies, deferred taxes (such as those on capital gains and registered plans) will have to be paid by the heirs. These expenses can significantly reduce the value of your estate. If your heirs will not immediately require the capital from your estate, a will allows some important tax-planning opportunities, such as creating trusts within the will.

- **Your life insurance**

  The best way to offset the costs of taxes and debts owing to your estate is by ensuring your life insurance is sufficient. Think ahead: if you predecease your spouse, would they need extra financial help to hire a caregiver or handle the burden of mortgage payments and maintenance costs? Factor these items into your life-insurance equation.

- **Your living will**

  Depending where you live, this may be referred to as a "power of attorney for personal care" or an "advanced health-care directive." This document deals with the personal and health-care decisions that need to be made in case you become incapacitated. Here you will outline your instructions, such as how to handle life-saving measures, organ donation, and ongoing care. A living will is important to help family members understand your wishes in critical situations and can reduce stress and strain in the most difficult of times.

- **Your executor**

  An executor, estate trustee, or liquidator is responsible for carrying out the terms of your will and settling your estate. Often a trusted professional advisor or a family member with legal or accounting expertise can be a good choice. Immediate family members, such as your spouse or children, need time to grieve and may be too emotionally concerned to handle the great amount of work and attention to detail required for this role.

- **Your guardian**

  If you have young kids, naming someone to look after their care is probably your greatest concern. Not only are you entrusting a legal guardian with the moral responsibility of raising your kids, you are also asking for major time and financial commitments. You may wish to secure a separate life-insurance policy or establish a trust account, which can be directed specifically to the care and education of your children.

- **Your philanthropy**

  You may wish to have part or all of your estate transferred to a charitable cause or structured as a foundation, which can disperse assets to various charities over time. You will need to appoint an administrator responsible for overseeing the appropriate disbursement of these funds.

## The Takeaway

Your spouse's and your wills, bequests, insurance policies, and trust arrangements are all key elements of your overall plan. With professional advice, you can design a complete estate plan that reflects your *values* and meets your *goals*.

**GOLDEN RULE: SHARE YOUR PLANS**

Talking through your plans with your spouse and family members will alleviate any surprises and help you to grant any specific wishes they may have with regard to your estate. Make sure your loved ones know about the documents in your estate plan and where to find them. You can provide them with copies for safekeeping and inform them of how to contact your lawyer who will keep copies on file for you.

And with that in place, you're done; you've laid the foundation. It's now time to work it, honey! Your retirement, that is . . .

# 9

## Ready to Launch

### *Finance and Next Steps*

### Baby, You Know You're Worth It

If there is one thought that we'd like to leave you with, it's that you *can* take control of your financial life. No matter how young you are, it is never too early to start. No matter how much wisdom of the ages you have accumulated, it is never too late to make up for lost time.

Actually, make that two thoughts: you *can* take control of your financial life and by doing so, you *will* change your entire life for the better.

That sounds like a very bold statement. We're prepared to stand behind it. In fact, we wanted to put it across the cover in bright red block letters ("This Book Will Change Your Life!"), but we thought that might scare you off.

Each of us involved with researching and writing this book has managed to take control and grab hold of the reins of her financial life and—hooray!—her financial power. Now that doesn't mean we're perfect (far from it), and some of us are certainly better than others (case in point: one of us spends *way* too much at a national drugstore chain in an effort to amass record-high levels of loyalty points), but the point is, we're on the path, we're on the journey, and we're holding on tight. (*Hey, get your hands off my money!*)

"But you're 'experts'," you might protest?! Well, yes, theoretically. We certainly know what we *should* do, but our propensity to actually follow through on every rule is a work in progress, as it is with any of us. We're only human, after all. Ever go to a doctor who just came back from a smoke break (after inhaling fast food, no less)? Or a hairstylist who hastily fashioned her bed-head hair with a banana clip and headed to work? You get the picture.

Indeed, our motivation for writing this book was to share our experiences, to be blunt, real, and authentic, and to get you *engaged* (and we don't mean with a big fat ring). To get you in the financial game, sweetheart!

You know you *should* get in the game. Yes, taking better care of your finances is one of those things you know you're supposed to do, like eating raw vegetables or spending more time with your cousins. And while you may have given up on crudités and second cousins Phil and Margaret years ago, by virtue of reading this book, you've taken one very big step in expressing a desire to master that golden area of your life (i.e., *money!*). In fact, you likely already know much of the information we've covered in these pages. A lot of it is common sense. A lot of it is stuff your parents may have nagged you about, or a financial advisor may have taught you along the way. (But how much of it did you remember? Or rather, how much did you actually put into practice over the years?) Hmmm . . .

You know you *should* be saving more, spending less, and investing something for the future. If you're like most women, you've had moments of panic at the thought of suddenly losing your job or being stricken ill and not being able to cover your rent, take care of your kids, or pay for medical bills. What woman, in the dark of night, hasn't imagined herself ending up alone, penniless, and eating cat food? (Weird but true. Remember that bag-lady phobia from Chapter 2?) There is no shortage of ominous financial statistics and horrifying news stories of financial wipeouts to leave you shaking in your stilettos. Yet, there always seems to be something else to do with your money, something more pressing. Why is it so hard to get started?

Getting control of your finances and taking the steps toward building wealth must be about more than just fear. There is no question that fear is a great motivator, but in our experience, danger has to be pretty much imminent, threatening to take everything away, in order for fear to truly give you a swift kick in the skirt.

In order for you to change your behaviour and take the steps toward controlling this area of your life, you have to really *want* to do it. Not just want it in your head, intellectually. Want it in *your bones*. You have to *sense* how you will feel at the outcome. You have to be ready. And you have to think ahead.

Because make no mistake, life has a very annoying way of sneaking up on you. (Here come those curveballs again.) You know, that honeymoon baby that is actually triplets; your employer abruptly closing up shop; that "dream fiancé" taking off with most of your wedding fund; or your attempt at entrepreneurship getting off to a bit of a slow start (oops). With all of these experiences (and many more, no doubt), your finances will ebb and flow. Rest assured, this is okay, and happens to the best of us. The real point is that being aware and active in your finances will help you to negotiate the ups, downs, and wonderful experiences that life has to offer. Not only does this awareness provide security for you and your family, it also gives you a toolkit complete with knowledge and your trusted advisors to help you face and navigate whatever life brings. It's about making a change . . . before you need to.

So with that said, let's look at some of the outcomes that might motivate you to make such a change. When you recognize the right reason for you, you won't just know it, you will *feel* it. Trust this instinct.

## 1. Achievement

If you have a history of wondering where your money goes, never having enough, or being afraid to use your money for fear of being without it, gaining control over your money will give you a remarkable sense of achievement and empowerment.

Suppose you have a goal to set up a life-insurance account that will sufficiently safeguard your estate, or a goal to commit an extra $200 a month to reducing your debt. At first, paying the premiums or making the debt payment will feel like a sacrifice. But each month, it will get a little bit easier and become part of your routine. Your spending will adjust around the missing cash until it feels normal. You will feel healthy; you will feel a sense of achievement by the very process alone.

Psychologically, you are teaching yourself that you can make a plan and stick to it. (You may be great at sticking to plans when it comes to caring for family or work responsibilities, but when it comes to a personal goal for yourself, it's often another story, right?) As each month goes by, you may even find yourself feeling stronger and more capable of making incremental changes in other areas of your life such as drinking less coffee or going for a 20-minute run after work.

After several months or a year, when you look at the financial statement that shows the cumulative effect of your small but consistent efforts, you will feel a burst of accomplishment and the pride that comes from self-care. You will have built faith in your own ability to set personal goals and to achieve them. Next goal? *Bring it on.*

## 2. Independence

We know a woman (and maybe you do, too) who moved from her childhood bedroom in her parents' home straight into her first house with her husband. She was a smart woman in her mid 20s, university-educated, and she and her husband both had solid, well-paying jobs.

However, when out strolling through a department store with a girlfriend one day, the woman became paralyzed at the lipstick counter. She had been trying on colours and now she held the box of her intended purchase in her hand. She shook her head, set the lipstick down on the counter, and walked away. The friend was confused; this woman had always spent her money prudently, rarely splurged, and, by all indications, had never lacked for cash or credit cards. The woman knew her girlfriend was waiting for an explanation and she finally turned to her and said, "It's just that, it's *our* money now. I'm sure my husband wouldn't mind, but I can't just go and spend it on myself anymore."

The girlfriend, who was not yet married (okay, it was one of us!), was left wondering, "Does marriage mean never being able to buy your own lipstick?"

Ladies, it was a $15 *lipstick*. (Okay, not as cheap as drugstore brands, but a tube of lipstick lasts for like a year! We're talking about pennies a day here.) Now, as you know, we are all for financial restraint and maybe the woman and her husband had committed to a strict budget in order to pay down the mortgage on their new house or plan for a family. Great, right? However, this was not the case.

When the couple married, they combined their credit cards and bank accounts. Guess who was in charge of balancing the chequebook, monitoring the account activity, paying the bills, and making the investments every month? Hint: not her. It isn't that this woman's husband was a control freak; she had just never handled bills or investments before, so it seemed logical to let him take care of it all. And she just wasn't in the mood to start defending "another" lipstick on the bank statement, when she had a dozen tubes already. Frankly, who can blame her?

But we digress. This is not a story about lipstick. This is an example of how easily and readily we women relinquish our control and independence (even over our own hard-earned income!) when someone else comes along and is willing to take over. If and when this woman's husband suddenly kicked the bucket or took off to "find himself," she would have no idea what bills to pay, what investments they had, or how much it costs to run the household.

Between singlehood, divorce, and death, there is a very good chance that at some point in your life—maybe a short time or perhaps longer than you expect—you will be on your own. Teamwork is a wonderful thing, but relying on someone else to handle your personal finances while you sail through life blindly is not just foolish, it is eventually debilitating.

Learn the basics, get involved, be an equal partner, and buy your own damn lipstick.

### 3. Freedom

You don't need to win the lottery to understand financial freedom (lovely as that would be). Debt is a ball and chain! While some debt is necessary (such as a mortgage), it ties you to onerous interest payments and restricts your opportunity to invest in yourself and your future. When you live paycheque to paycheque, you do not feel free. Your stress is high, your choices are restricted, and you live in fear of any minor setbacks. Any extra cost such as a flat tire, an unexpected tax bill, or the dog getting sick can throw you into a financial tailspin.

The emotional security that comes from having savings in the bank and being debt-free gives you an enormous amount of freedom. Freedom from sleepless nights. Freedom from creditor calls. Freedom to walk away from a bad situation. Freedom to enjoy going to work because you love your job. Freedom to fearlessly change jobs or switch careers. Most of all, freedom to make choices for yourself.

### 4. Opportunity

Your BFF just won an all-inclusive stay at a luxury resort in Turks and Caicos and she wants you to join her! Fantastic—if only your credit card wasn't maxed out, you could pay for your airfare. Or, the cottage you've been lusting after for 20 years is finally on the market, but you're too heavily leveraged to qualify for another mortgage. Or, you're downsized from a job you hated anyway, but you can't afford to take time off and go back to school for the interior-design course that would kick-start the career of your dreams.

Those little Boy Scouts with their motto of "Be prepared" are definitely onto something. Life brings all kinds of unexpected crises, but it also has a beautiful way of bringing unexpected opportunities—and if we're not financially prepared to take advantage of them, we can easily miss out.

You know your heart's desire. Ask yourself: if it knocked on your door right now, would you be prepared to grab it— emotionally *and* financially?

### 5. Worth

You would never judge someone by his or her net worth, so why should you be concerned about your own? Knowing your own net worth and working to systematically improve it, year after year, can be a master booster to your sense of self-worth. Why? Net worth cuts through the little lies we tell ourselves and lays bare the true health of our financial position. By knowing precisely where you are at, you can make better decisions to build your wealth, protect your lifestyle, and achieve the future you desire a little bit at a time, year by year.

You may think that those Joneses, living in the million-dollar home down the street, are so much better off than you. But what you don't see is how much debt they may be servicing to pay for that enormous house, posh furniture, and luxury cars. Some of the wealthiest-looking people you know may actually have a negative net worth. You may have fewer acquisitions to show for it, but if you have a positive net worth, you are in far better financial shape than your so-called millionaire neighbour. And that bodes very well for your future.

There is another reason for measuring your net worth regularly. When you apply for a mortgage or a loan, banks will check your net worth as a first step in checking your eligibility. Clearly they would view someone who owns more than they owe as less of a risk. If you suddenly stopped making your loan payments, they would expect you to sell your assets to come up with the money. On the other hand, if you owe more than you own, a lender would consider you a higher risk, as they'd probably have to get in line with your other creditors in order to collect from you.

Are you ready to try it? The calculation is simple:

$$assets - liabilities = net\ worth$$

This basic metric will give you a sense of your overall financial health. If you calculate your net worth on an annual basis, you will have a fairly good indication of your overall financial stability and progress. Even if you start out with a negative net worth right now, by working to improve it each year, you will build your confidence and self-esteem. It's like doing anything healthy for yourself (going to the gym, eating a nutritious breakfast); it takes a bit of effort, but you feel so good about yourself afterward.

## How to Calculate Your Net Worth

### Step 1: Know your assets from your liabilities

Your assets come in three varieties:

- **Cash and investments:** Also referred to as your "liquid assets"—and this does not mean the bottle of Patrón Gold tequila in your freezer. It does include everything in your chequing and savings accounts, that stash of cash you keep under your mattress, any unregistered investments, GICs, stocks, bonds, mutual funds, and that money your sister still owes you.

- **Long-term assets:** You probably also have investments registered in your name that are tied up in such a way that you can't access the funds on a whim (no matter how hard you may have tried). For example, registered retirement plans, pension plans, and life-insurance policies.

- **Hard assets:** Despite your diligent work on the Stairmaster, we're not talking about your enviable bottom. (Stay focused on your bottom *line* here.) Hard assets, also known as "property assets" include your home, vehicles, boats, jewellery, artwork, antiques, collectibles, furnishings, home electronics, appliances, and any other valuable item that you imagine selling in order to buy a crumbling nineteenth-century villa under the Tuscan sun.

Your liabilities include any money that you owe:

- **Make a list of all your debts,** including the mortgage on your home, student loans, credit-card debt, personal loans, lines of credit, department-store cards, unpaid taxes, the lovely patio furniture you "bought now" and for which you promised to "pay later," and the cash you borrowed from your parents in order to lend money to your sister (they always loved you best, we know).

### Step 2: The calculation

Add up the monetary value of all your assets to get your total assets. Then, (don't be scared) add up the value of all your debt to get your total liabilities.

Now subtract your total liabilities from your total assets—voila! This is your net worth.

Do you get a negative number or a positive number? Ideally the number (and therefore your net worth) will be positive. For many, especially those who have recently bought a home and have a big mortgage ahead of them, this may be a negative net worth. Your challenge is to keep this number moving in a *positive direction*, slowly and steadily, up, up, up.

### Step 3: Give your net worth a boost

The following are a few strategies to help you boost your assets and reduce your liabilities. Kind of like a girdle for your personal finances.

- Pay off your mortgage as quickly as possible, increasing your payment schedule if you can. This will lower your liabilities, while the increasing market value of your home will give your assets a boost.

- Continue to pay off outstanding loans, personal debts, and eliminate credit-card debt by reducing your spending (yes, you can!).

- Pay off your car loans as soon as you can, with the goal of reducing your liability faster than the value of your car depreciates.

- Put your savings into investments that provide dividends or income flow.

- The earlier you start investing, the more compound interest will grow your principal and therefore the value of your assets.

The great thing about calculating your net worth is that it doesn't take a financial degree to figure it out and you can do it in the privacy of your own backyard, reclining on your chaise longue, with a margarita in one hand and calculator in the other. Mm-hmm . . . you *know* you're worth it!

## Go Forth and Prosper

Well, ladies, that's all we have for you—for now. Know that we are always just a click away at GoldenGirlFinance.ca where you will find tons of articles, a comprehensive glossary of financial terms (in that "golden" voice, of course), Q&As, and up-to-the-minute information to keep you enlightened, informed, and in control of your personal finances.

Better still, sign up for our free weekly financial e-newsletters to read about media stories with a financial spin (*mais oui!*) and very savvy end-of-the-week market updates. Think unbiased, unbridled, and totally unique.

We hope you will use the information in this book and on our website to help you build your own wealth, protect it, invest it, and get your money working harder for *you*. Most of all, we hope you will feel more confident and less intimidated by the world of personal finance.

It may just be money, but it's *your* money, honey. Own it!

# Golden Girl Finance Club:
# Meeting Discussion Guide

## Tapping into the Sisterhood

While the content in this book is about your *personal* finances, Golden Girl Finance was created out of a desire to lift the veil on the way women handle their finances; to get us talking and sharing about money.

We women are legendary for sharing everything. When you get together with your girlfriends, is any topic too personal? When you were considering which form of birth control to use, to whom did you turn? Your mother? Your doctor? The Internet? All helpful, perhaps informative. But it was your girlfriends who gave you the lowdown on the *real* pros and cons from their own experiences.

Get a group of girls together and (if it's going well) the conversation will quickly digress to the dishiest of topics. What *really* happens to your body in the third trimester of pregnancy? How *do* you handle it when your husband's co-worker sends him flirty texts? What *kind* of bikini wax is appropriate these days? We love to share the wealth of our experiences. We love to seek and give advice. We love to learn the secrets that our sisters already know.

However, it seems as if finance is the one topic that gets left behind. Maybe it's because we don't think of ourselves as knowledgeable; maybe we think we'll be judged if our girlfriends find out we're not as financially organized as we may appear; maybe it's because we think it's boring.

Think about your best girlfriend for a moment. You probably know the name of her first major crush. You know about her miscarriage and how many times she and her husband did the business before they got pregnant. You know who cuts and colours her hair and what kind of cocktail she has vowed to never, ever drink again. You know about the time she almost got breast implants and the time she really did get a belly ring.

But do you know what her annual salary is? Do you know what the down payment was on her house? What her credit-card limit is? Do you know how much she has saved for retirement? Somehow, illogically, we seem to feel that our financial lives are off limits. Men, on the other hand . . .

## Lessons from the Menfolk

Men seem to have no reticence in swapping the details of their financial lives. Leave your man standing over a barbecue with another guy for half an hour and he will come back and be able to tell you the price the guy paid for his new house, how much money he made or lost in his mutual funds last year, and what he spent on his fiancée's engagement ring. Whether it's a lifelong pal or a guy he just met, makes little difference.

Of course, if you ask your man how the other guy *feels* about getting married, you'll probably get a half shrug and a look like you're crazy. For men, talking about money is easy. It's not emotional, it's not deep nor complicated. It's just money. So what's the big deal?

Men are open with each other about their finances in the same way that women are open about their sex lives, their grooming habits, and their health. They learn from each other. Men compare salaries, investments, and expenditures so they can determine what's average, what's normal, what's appropriate—what they can expect when they face the same milestones.

Ladies, we need to do this too. We have so much more that we can learn from one another. *Share!*

## The Golden Girl Finance Party Planner

So what's the best way to break the ice? With a great party, naturally!

From old-fashioned sewing circles to pre-wedding hen parties, women have historically gathered to socialize, build networks, care for children and family members, cook together, help out with homes and gardens, and share wisdom. And now, finally, to talk *finances*.

We've put together a bit of a planning guide to help you organize a fabulous Golden Girl Finance party.

✓ **The guest list**

Think of it like planning a book club or a shower. You want to invite enough women to create a festive, lively group, yet not so many that you can't have a cohesive group discussion. Anywhere from 5 to 15 is probably appropriate. A great idea: ask women who span multiple generations, from gals in their 20s to women in their 60s and 70s, to attend. A little hindsight and foresight is good for us all.

✓ **The experts**

Invite a financial advisor to give a short chat to kick off the discussion. By meeting *regularly* (key to being accountable and consistent, akin to stepping on that financial scale), you can focus the topic on different areas of financial planning and invite a different expert for each. For example, household budgeting, buying real estate, the stock market, teaching kids financial responsibility, life insurance, tax planning, wills and estates, or salaries. The one rule: full disclosure!

### ✓ The twenty-first-century golden girls

Yes, thank you, we'd *love* to come to your party! E-mail info@goldengirlfinance.ca and let us know about your get-together. One of our trusted experts, supporters, or maybe even authors Laura and Susan ourselves will do their best to (virtually) meet your friends and join your group via Skype to help you kick off your discussion.

### ✓ The music

Set the mood with girl-power grooves: maybe Estelle, Adele, Joss Stone, or Carla Bruni (for a little *je ne sais quoi* flair). We like Gwen Stefani's "Rich Girl," too. *Obviously.*

### ✓ The Three Ps

In our experience, the surefire, no-fail plan for an excellent evening (or afternoon) with the girls includes the three Ps: Prosecco, pizza, and pie.

1. **Prosecco** makes for an elegant, bubbly (and much cheaper!) alternative to champagne. Perfect for girls' get-togethers. Serve it straight up or try mixing up your own version of a Money Honey Cocktail to get the conversation flowing. (We suggest a homemade honey-ginger syrup mixed with Prosecco. Throw in a piece of crystallized ginger . . . looks like a gold nugget, no?)

2. **Pizza** keeps things simple and is the secret indulgence of every woman (bread and cheese, *oh yes!*). Order from your favourite shop or buy frozen thin-crust Napolitano-style pizzas. Slice into squares and lay out on serving platters for a steady supply of *molto delizioso* highly munchable finger food.

3. **Pie**, but not just any pie. This is a celebration: you are cracking the code on women and their finances! Your guests will have earned a sweet reward, so treat them accordingly, but honey, don't kill yourself in the kitchen over it. We find that Champagne Truffle Pie is our go-to dessert for instant wow factor and practically no cooking skills are required. (You can find the super-easy recipe at annamagazine.ca.)

## ✓ The agenda

Once everyone has arrived, with cocktail in hand and pizza passed, assemble all in a loosely circular area. You can meet over the kitchen table or the backyard patio; we find that "sitting soft" in a low-lit living room makes things cozy. Turn the music down as a signal to get started.

- Thank everyone for coming, then introduce your theme and discussion for the night (or afternoon). Invite your speaker to chat for 20 to 30 minutes, offering tips and stories from her own experience.

- Use our list of conversation starters that follow. You may have to jump in first with your own anecdotes and questions to get things going.

- If you have a particularly chatty group (you *know* who you are), use a kitchen hourglass timer to give everyone talking limits.

- After 45 to 60 minutes of discussion, bring out the pie and offer coffee or tea. Turn the music back up and let the conversation flow where it may.

## ✓ The swag

What's a party without a loot bag? Order copies of *It's Your Money, Honey* for a special group discount price by contacting us at info@goldengirlfinance.ca

✓ Follow up

Send out a post-party e-mail sharing contact information for all the guests who may wish to stay in touch. We suggest you set a date and venue for the next gathering or ask for volunteers to host the next one. Better still, start a Golden Girl Finance Club! (You'll find a full list of chapter questions to fuel the discussion in the pages that follow.) Just make sure to keep the party going, say monthly or quarterly. It's about gathering up your girlfriends and forming a financial community—your own circle of financially savvy friends. Let the men eat cake; you've got your champagne pie!

## Conversation Starters

Use some of the following conversation starters to go around the room and let everyone share their experiences. If you are focusing your group on a particular area of personal finance, your conversation starters will obviously vary. Do your own brainstorming beforehand to make sure you are prepared with lots of questions and sub-topics.

1. What was your first money memory as a child?

2. In one word, describe your attitude toward your finances.

3. What was your "wealthiest" moment?

4. What would you do if you realized you had an extra $1,000 this month?

5. What's the best investment you ever made? The worst?

6. Name one thing you learned from your parents about money.

7. Do you know your net worth?

8. How much money do you put into savings each month?

9. Do you pay off your credit card in full each month or carry a balance?

10. Do you have a will? An estate plan?

11. Have you planned your retirement?

12. How do you teach your kids about being responsible with money?

13. What is your current salary (and bonus, and commission) and what have been your salaries leading up to it? (Of course, this can be in general or more specific terms, as much as everyone feels comfortable sharing, which we hope will be *plenty!*)

## Chapter Questions (chapters 1 to 8)

### Chapter 1: The First Taste of Freedom

1. Where did you live when you were starting out? Did you stay at home, move in with friends, or get your own place? What were your main expenses?

2. What lessons did you learn from your first experience moving out? Looking back, is there anything you would do differently?

3. Did you have a job as a young adult? What lessons did you learn during your first days of employment?

4. How did you manage your money when you were starting out? Did you have a budget, pool your money with friends, tap into the Bank of Parents, or hope for the best?

5. Did you take a gap year? If so, describe your experiences and whether or not they were worthwhile. Did your gap year move you forward or set you back, in terms of finances?

6. What choices did you make when pursuing an education? Did you attend school full-time, part-time, or delay your education? Did you attend school close to home or move away?

7. How did you finance your education? Did you work, receive help from family, win scholarships, or get student loans?

8. When did you receive your first credit card or credit facility? What were some of your first experiences with credit?

9. Have a look at "Sowing the Seeds of Your Self-Sufficiency." How would you rate your own progress on this list? What is the most important next step you should take to become more financially self-sufficient?

10. Looking back, what financial advice would you give a young woman who is just starting out?

## Chapter 2: Love, Relationships, and Money

1. Do you ever fear losing it all, in terms of your money and possessions? When do you feel most vulnerable?

2. What are some of your earliest memories about earning money (and spending it)? Did you feel secure, grateful, fearful, guilty, anxious, or something else?

3. How have your earliest feelings about money impacted your life? Are you a spender, saver, or something in between?

4. How would you describe your financial relationship with your partner? Is finance and money something you discuss on a regular basis, periodic basis, or never? How satisfied are you with this arrangement?

5. Do you have a distinct breadwinner in your family? If so, is it you or your partner? Does this cause any friction or challenges with handling your joint finances? How do you resolve concerns about who pays for what? What do you do to ensure both of you feel valued for the contributions you each make?

6. How would you describe your level of involvement in managing your finances as a couple or family? Do you take the lead role, help out, or rely on someone else to manage the finances

and make financial decisions? How satisfied are you with this arrangement?

7. Are you a candidate for a cohabitation or pre-nuptial agreement? If so, what are your feelings around entering into this type of agreement? What steps could you take to get some assistance in this area?

8. Are you planning a wedding? What financial decisions will you make for your big day? Have you set a budget, made trade-offs, or are you planning a big splash?

9. What are some things you find work well when managing money or making financial decisions in a relationship? What doesn't work well?

10. What are some of the financial experiences you have had in times of relationship breakdowns, such as the breakup of a long-term relationship or divorce? What is the most important lesson you have learned?

## Chapter 3: For the Love of Those Little Cost Creatures

1. Review "The Three Truths of Motherhood." How do you feel about the importance of these areas? If you are a mother, how would you rate yourself in each area?

2. Have you taken steps to protect your family's or children's financial requirements? Do you have life, disability, or critical-illness insurance?

3. Do you have a will? If so, what did you learn from creating it? If not, what is one thing you could do to get started?

4. Have you appointed a guardian for your children? If so, what was your decision process? If not, what is one thing you could do to get started in appointing a guardian?

5. How is the money managed in your household? Is your current arrangement working, not working?

6. What is the most important thing you need to do to improve how money is managed and financial decisions are made in your household?

7. Are you part of a blended family? If so, what are some financial challenges you have faced? What are some things that have worked well, in terms of finances and managing money?

8. How much stuff do you think your kids really need? Are you guilty of giving too much? If so, why?

9. Have you taken steps to teach your kids about money? If so, what are some approaches that have worked well? Have not worked well?

10. What is the most important thing that you would like your children to understand about money? Have you taught them this lesson yet?

## Chapter 4: Building Your Dream Career

1. What was the first post-education, full-time job you had? What did you learn from that job?

2. Are you an employee or an independent contractor? In financial terms, do you understand the difference?

3. If you are an employee, do you understand how you are paid? Gross salary, net salary, deductions?

4. Are you a member of a group benefits plan? What type of coverage do you have? Do you understand how the plan works?

5. Are you a member of a pension plan? What is the structure of the plan? Do you understand how the plan works?

6. Do you consider the amount of money you earn to be fair for the job you do? Why or why not?

7. Are you aware of comparable compensation for your position? Have you looked at salary surveys, other similar job postings, or asked around?

8. Would you be comfortable approaching your company for a pay raise if you felt an increase was justified? If so, what would you say?

9. Have you ever received a severance package? If so, what did you learn from that experience?

10. What are some ways that you could use your employment knowledge to advance your career or to build something for yourself?

**Chapter 5: So Crazy, It Just Might Work**

1. Are you (or are you planning to be) a business owner? What type of business are you in? Why did you choose to go into business for yourself?

2. Is your business a proprietorship, partnership, or corporation? Why did you choose this particular structure? Do you understand the differences between these structures?

3. Do you have a business plan, including a financial forecast, for your business? Why or why not?

4. Does your business require financing from outside investors or financial partners? Do know how much money you require and why?

5. Have you approached potential financial partners to provide capital to your business? If so, what has been their response? If not, what is holding you back?

6. Is your business more focused on your own needs (i.e., a lifestyle business) or on the needs of the marketplace and customers? Are you comfortable with the focus of your business and its ability to meet your financial needs for the long term?

7. Are you concerned about competitive pressures in the marketplace that could result in your business losing customers? What are some steps you could take to decrease this risk?

8. Is your business just you, or do you have employees or partners working with you? What are your short- and long-term goals in terms of financial and employment growth?

9. How well does your business operate? Are your employees well trained, motivated, and self-sufficient, or is improvement required in this area?

10. What are your long-term plans for the business? If you plan to transfer the business to someone else, do you actually have something to sell, or is the business dependent on you? What steps could you take to reduce this dependency?

## Chapter 6: The Big-Ticket Items of Life

1. Have you purchased (or are you planning to purchase) a home or condo? Have you set a budget? How did you determine your budget?

2. Do you have a down payment to purchase a residence? Is your down payment in the bank, partially saved, or not yet started? What steps could you take to save the down payment that you require?

3. Have you started to shop for a mortgage? What types of mortgages are you considering? Do you understand the differences between these types of mortgages?

4. As a homeowner, how have you managed the financial requirements of your home, such as mortgage payments, maintenance, and renovation costs? How well has your approach worked?

5. Have you undertaken renovation projects on your home? In financial terms, what are some things that worked well? Did not work well?

6. Review "The Five Cs of an Attractive Borrower." Would you consider yourself to be an attractive candidate for a loan? How would you rate yourself and your major purchase in terms of capacity, capital, collateral, character, and credit?

7. If you are currently renting a house or apartment, what are your plans for the future? Do you want to own a residence at some point? What steps do you need to take to get there?

8. Do you have a car? Is it new or used? Is it owned outright, financed, or shared? What was your financial decision-making process when acquiring your car?

9. Do you have (or are you considering purchasing) a vacation property? What is your financial plan for acquiring and owning a vacation property?

10. Do you have (or are you considering purchasing) an investment property? What is your financial plan for acquiring and owning an investment property?

## Chapter 7: Making Your Money Work for You

1. Do you have a financial advisor to manage your money? How did you find your advisor?

2. Has your financial advisor worked with you to develop an investment plan? How comfortable are you with the plan?

3. Do you manage your money yourself, perhaps through an on-line brokerage? What have you found the benefits and challenges of this approach to be?

4. How would you describe the mix of your investment portfolio? What level of risk are you willing to accept and why?

5. Do you own any public-company stocks directly? Why did you choose these particular stocks? Do you follow the developments of these companies in the media?

6. Do you understand the difference between *dividends* and *returns* (i.e., appreciation)? Do you have any investments that pay dividends?

7. Do you own any bonds in your investment portfolio? Do you prefer this type of investment structure to public-company stocks?

8. Do you understand how your advisor charges you for their service? Fees, commissions, or some type of blended arrangement?

9. Are you satisfied with the job that your financial advisor is doing? Are you making sufficient progress on your investment plan? Do you have an opportunity to evaluate or provide feedback to your financial advisor?

10. What is the most important lesson you have learned in working with a financial advisor?

## Chapter 8: The Best Third of Your Life

1. Have you thought about your retirement? How would you describe the vision you have for your retirement?

2. What are your financial dreams and fears, in terms of retirement? Are there steps you could take to reduce your fears?

3. Review "Getting Started: Age-Appropriate Tips." Find your age category and comment on how well you are progressing. What are some things you could do to improve?

4. Is your current retirement plan your kids, your husband, or your house? Do you understand the limitations of these approaches? What are some steps you could take to get on a more self-sufficient path?

5. What do you expect the sources of your retirement income to be? Investments, company pensions, government pensions, or employment income? Are there any additional sources of income that you could generate?

6. What is your real-estate plan for retirement? Do you plan to stay in your residence, downsize, share accommodations, or move? How would this plan impact your finances?

7. Have you ever considered securing a reverse mortgage on your home? Do you have friends who have taken this approach, and what were their thoughts on the pros and cons of this cash-flow option?

8. Review "What If I Don't Have Enough to Retire?" Which approaches would you be the most comfortable adopting and why?

9. Do you have an estate plan? Does your plan require updating or addition of key information, such as powers of attorney and charitable giving?

10. What would you like your legacy to be? What does *legacy* mean to you, in financial terms?

## About Golden Girl Finance

Photo by Izabela Rachwal

Golden Girl Finance believes that every girl needs a financial best friend. Launched in July 2010, GoldenGirlFinance.ca has quickly become the most fun, fresh, and thoroughly modern on-line financial resource for women in Canada today. Born out of the notion that too many smart women let their financial situation be ignored, swept under the rug, or dictated by others, the goal of Golden Girl Finance has been to rebrand finance with a feminine spin to engage women of all ages to take a greater interest—and play a greater role—in those financial issues that affect their everyday lives and financial futures. It is about wealth creation, wealth management, and financial protection as it relates to women personally and to their families. And it's all done on-line via a content-rich website and valuable weekly e-mail campaigns, acting as an agent of leverage for women's very busy lives.

For more info, please visit: www.GoldenGirlFinance.ca.

# About the Authors

Photo by David A. Brown

## Laura J. McDonald
### Co-Founder, Golden Girl Finance Inc.

Passionate, driven, and trend-focused, Laura is an entrepreneur, writer, and communications and brand consultant. She is also the co-founder of GoldenGirlFinance.ca, Canada's most innovative on-line financial literacy resource for women today.

Laura brings an entrepreneur's stance to Golden Girl Finance, while offering the outsider's take of the financial world. As a smart, educated woman—who, like many, was at one time prone to leave all the financial details up to her husband—Laura's goal is to make finance and the stock market an engaging and accessible part of women's everyday lives. Women need to think big, grow enterprises, and build wealth. Finance for women by women.

### Susan L. Misner

### Co-Founder, Golden Girl Finance Inc.

As a 20-year veteran of the wealth-management industry and co-founder of GoldenGirl Finance.ca, Susan has significant knowledge and expertise in all areas of the investment business. And while her mission as a consultant was always to work hard for her clients' money, her passion lies in a more holistic view of wealth management.

Photo by David A. Brown

With a firm belief in legacy planning for women, she is most inspired by her two young daughters, who instill in Susan a constant drive to make sure opportunities for women in finance—and the inclusion of women in financial discourse—remain top priorities in the investment landscape. Her mission is to make finance real, relevant, and relatable for women so they are better able to accumulate, grow, and protect their wealth. In her mind, the future of finance is female.

# About the Expert Contributors

We are honoured and privileged to have four incredibly talented and brilliant experts help in the creation of this book. These women understand the female voice, are driven to build female wealth, and have contributed their knowledge and expertise throughout every page of this book. Drum roll please . . .

Photo by David A. Brown

### Jenifer Bartman

### Founder and Principal, Jenifer Bartman Business Advisory Services

Jenifer Bartman assists companies that are undergoing transition, including growth, financing, succession, and performance improvement. An experienced senior executive, Jenifer was the vice-president and chief financial officer of ENSIS Management Inc., a venture capital fund manager, for more than nine years. She graduated from the University of Manitoba and holds the designations of Chartered Accountant and Certified Management Consultant.

The author of *Master Your Investment in the Family Business: How to Increase After-Tax Wealth*, Jenifer has written for various websites and magazines, including GoldenGirlFinance.ca, Yahoo! Finance, Private Capital, and Canadian Capital. She has also developed courses for national educational institutes and universities (The Knowledge Bureau and the University of Manitoba) in the areas of technology-commercialization management, business-succession planning, and business valuation for advisors.

Jenifer is actively involved with the Canadian Venture Capital Association and was recognized for her volunteer efforts as the inaugural recipient of the Intercontinental Hotels Group Canada 2007 CSTA Community Service Award, presented by the Canadian Sport Tourism Alliance.

### Stephanie Holmes-Winton

### President and CEO, The Money Finder

Stephanie Holmes-Winton is a Halifax-based advisor, author, speaker, radio columnist, and the president and chief executive officer of The Money Finder. She is on a self-appointed mission

Photo by Shari Tucker       to see that Canadians get the kind of financial advice they need—to get what they truly want and deserve from their money.

With this in mind, Stephanie advocates a healthy financial philosophy. She educates Canadians to help them avoid making "fear-based financial decisions." Showing people that money is less about math and more about meaning helps Stephanie lead the way to lasting financial change for her clients.

Stephanie's first book, *Defusing the Debt Bomb*, was followed by the launch of the companion blog, a resource for advisors ready to tackle debt and cash-flow challenges, both for themselves and for their clients. Her second book, *$pent*, aims to help readers determine their "money mindset" and change their financial behaviour by understanding *why* they do *what* with their money.

### Anna-Marie Lyons

### Financial Planning Consultant, RBC Dominion Securities

Anna-Marie Lyons brings a wealth of experience to her role as a financial planning consultant with RBC Dominion Securities in Vancouver. A graduate of the Ivey MBA program at the University of Western Ontario, she has partici-

Photo by Tamea Burd

pated in the wealth-management industry as an investment advisor, branch manager, financial planner, and financial divorce specialist. She thrives on the opportunity to help clients understand their money attitudes and why they can be a source of conflict, and has studied mediation and conflict resolution at the Justice Institute of British Columbia.

With three young adult daughters, Anna-Marie has had many years of practice in engaging young women in financial education so that they can make informed financial decisions. She is an advocate of lifelong learning about finance, starting with open conversations in the home and inclusion in the school system.

### Rachel E. R. Margolis

### Lawyer (Corporate and Commercial Law), Aikins, MacAulay & Thorvaldson LLP

Rachel was called to the bar in 1997 and practises primarily in the area of corporate and commercial law with an emphasis on corporate

Photo by David A. Brown

reorganizations, business and succession planning, trust and estate planning, and real-estate law.

She is a member of the Society of Trust and Estate Practitioners, the Law Society of Manitoba, the Manitoba Bar Association, and the Canadian Bar Association.

As a working mother of three school-age children, she identifies with women who need to find that comfort zone between career, family, and friends, and also understands how significantly a young family can affect your estate-planning needs. She works very closely with clients to ensure all facets of their legal life are in order—whether it be through estate planning, business growth and succession, or clients going through separation or divorce.

# Index

CPSIA information can be obtained at www.ICGtesting.com
Printed in the USA
BVOW05s0416270315

393539BV00004B/16/P